Praise for the original edition:

"This book . . . may be just the foot in the door that will open up new possibilities to a teen in emotional trouble." —*KLIATT*

"Its honest, anecdote-filled treatment of the subject . . . make [the book] a no-brainer to buy." —*Youthworker*

"The most positive book on depression one could read . . . should be available to all teens." —*VOYA*

When Nothing Matters Anymore

revised & updated edition

When Nothing Matters Anymore

a survival guide for depressed teens

by Bev Cobain, R.N.,C.
Edited by Elizabeth Verdick

free spirit
PUBLiSHiNG®

Helping kids
help themselves™
since 1983

Library of Congress Cataloging-in-Publication Data
Cobain, Bev, 1940–
    When nothing matters anymore : a survival guide for depressed teens / by Bev Cobain ; edited by Elizabeth Verdick.
        p. cm.
    ISBN-13: 978-1-57542-235-0
    ISBN-10: 1-57542-235-2
1. Depression in adolescence—Juvenile literature. I. Verdick, Elizabeth. II. Title
    RJ506.D4C6 2007
    618.92'8527—dc22
                                                            2006036325

At the time of this book's publication, all facts and figures cited are the most current available. All telephone numbers, addresses, and Web site URLs are accurate and active; all publications, organizations, Web sites, and other resources exist as described in this book; and all have been verified as of November 2006. The author and Free Spirit Publishing make no warranty or guarantee concerning the information and materials given out by organizations or content found at Web sites, and we are not responsible for any changes that occur after this book's publication. If you find an error or believe that a resource listed here is not as described, please contact Free Spirit Publishing. Parents, teachers, and other adults: We strongly urge you to monitor children's use of the Internet.

Note to Readers: This book contains general information and advice about depression. It should not replace professional medical and psychiatric treatment.

The painting on the cover is by Kurt Cobain at age thirteen. Used with permission.

Cover design: Marieka Heinlen
Interior design: Michelle Lee
Illustrator: Jeff Tolbert

10 9 8 7 6 5 4 3 2 1
Printed in United States of America

Free Spirit Publishing Inc.
217 Fifth Avenue North, Suite 200
Minneapolis, MN 55401-1299
(612) 338-2068
help4kids@freespirit.com
www.freespirit.com

 Printed on recycled paper
including 30%
post-consumer waste

Free Spirit Publishing is a member of the Green Press Initiative, and we're committed to printing our books on recycled paper containing a minimum of 30% post-consumer waste (PCW). For every ton of books printed on 30% PCW recycled paper, we save 5.1 trees, 2,100 gallons of water, 114 gallons of oil, 18 pounds of air pollution, 1,230 kilowatt hours of energy, and .9 cubic yards of landfill space. At Free Spirit it's our goal to nurture not only young people, but nature too!

 green press INITIATIVE

Dedication

For Darren and Michael

Acknowledgments

I acknowledge:	for helping as my:
Anna Kurkoski, R.N.	inspiration to write this book
Karin and Bob Rose	friends and electronic benefactors
Bob Getz	friend, chauffeur, and taskmaster
Jane Whitney	friend and stabilizing force
Bernie Gilroy, ARNP	friend and colleague
Pat Tarner	pointer-outer of shoddy sentences
Seattle Mental Health	teen interview resource
Terry Douglass, Ph.D.	colleague and teen resource
Betty Hopper, M.D.	personal mental health advisor
Free Spirit Publishing	means of getting my message to teens

To Elizabeth Verdick, my editor: You kept me working long past my bedtime to meet impossible deadlines, then woke me up too darned early in the morning with more of your amazing ideas. You challenged me to think beyond the limits of my original objectives. You suggested creative ways to present difficult material. Most importantly, you taught me that writing a book, like getting through life, requires hard work, persistence, an open mind, loving support, and encouragement; it's a team effort. Thank you, and Free Spirit, for being part of my team.

Special gratitude for the unbelievable help I received from the staff of the Adolescent Treatment Unit of Kitsap Mental Health Services in Bremerton, Washington. I also thank my friends, family, workmates, and members of my community, who supported me with encouragement, material, suggestions, and interviews.

I also thank the following people for reading my manuscript and offering suggestions: Dr. Peter Lewinsohn, Adjunct Professor of Psychiatry at the Oregon Health Sciences University in Portland; Dr. Boris Birmaher, University of Pittsburgh Medical Center; Sue Eastgard, M.S.W., Director, Youth Suicide Prevention Program for Washington State; Christine Harnack, Licensed Psychologist, Volunteers of America of Minnesota, Mental Health Clinics; and Thomas S. Greenspon, Ph.D., Licensed Psychologist.

Most of all, I thank you wounded teens who touched and inspired me with your pain, your courage, your healing, and your willingness to let me "put it all out there" so that your wounded comrades may believe that their lives absolutely do matter.

P.S. It has been impossible to stay in touch with all of the teens who shared their original stories in the first edition of this book, as they are now out in the world living their lives. Happily, though, I have located five of them who brought me up to date on their current circumstances and were pleased to share their success stories with me.

DAVID, now twenty-eight, suffered from severe anxiety and depression as a teen, and once planned his suicide. He finds that his daily antidepressant therapy has completely eradicated the symptoms that used to torture him. He no longer sees a therapist because he has learned to better cope with his problems and to look at his life more positively.

HEIDI, now twenty-five, feels that she has come a long way since she shared her story in the original book. One of the first things she said to me was, "I hope that when I have kids they are never as brutal to me as I was to my parents. Having loving parents made a big difference in how my life has turned out." She believes that therapy and medication helped her learn to have more patience with herself and others. She is married and having a "good" life.

HEATHER, twenty-three, is enjoying her college classes in creative writing. Because bipolar illness doesn't just disappear, Heather must take medication every day, and if she forgets or decides not to take her meds for a few days, she says that the mania is the first effect she notices. She admits that having to depend on medication to feel well is sometimes overwhelming, but she says that the depression and mania are worse. She occasionally visits the campus therapist when the need arises.

SHAWNELLE, who's now twenty-eight, spent much of her spare time during and after high school doing volunteer work with kids in her church, and she says this gave her positive feelings about herself. Today, she has no signs of depression or suicidal thoughts, and she doesn't take medications or see a therapist at this time. She experiences the same ups and downs as everyone else but reminds herself that she can get through anything now. "I would like to tell other depressed teens that it's nice to have friends your own age to confide in, but problems get solved faster when you talk to someone with more life experience and wisdom."

MACKENZIE remained on antidepressants and continued therapy for a long while after writing her original story for the book. Talking things over with her therapist taught her that negative thinking was a factor in her depression. She graduated from college with no further bouts of depression until she experienced a major loss, at which time she began having panic attacks; her therapist again prescribed an antidepressant. "I really utilized my parents and friends during this time," Mackenzie told me. "I was shocked to realize that even though I might feel fine one minute, the depression was always waiting in the wings to return." Now twenty-five, Mackenzie plans to start law school this year. "For me," she says, "my support system is priceless. I no longer feel alone, ignored, or unworthy of happiness. Everyone deserves to feel happy— some just have to work harder at it."

Contents

Part 1: What's Wrong?

Part 2: Getting Help and Staying Well

Foreword

This survival guide, now in a well-deserved and much needed second edition, is a remarkable resource for young people with depression. Author Bev Cobain is cousin to Kurt Cobain, who was the lead singer of the rock band Nirvana when he tragically took his own life in 1994. Because popular figures like Kurt Cobain are so important and looked up to by youth, the question "Why did he do it?" is inevitably raised. Moreover, the question *should* be raised, because people with depression, young and old alike, frequently ask basic questions about the value and meaning of life—and rightly or wrongly, they often turn to people they admire to find answers. Yet sometimes, potential role models choose incorrectly, as Kurt Cobain did, with consequences that leave in their wake a continuing cycle of confusion and despair for those left behind. Thus, other role models are needed—role models with the courage to come forward and provide another end to the story. They can help depressed teens realize they aren't alone, others have felt as they do, help is available, and trained help given in a timely fashion works.

Bev Cobain understands and has felt the confusion of family and friends who are left behind after suicide. But she hasn't allowed her own story to end there. Instead, she has gathered the stories of teens—role models for depressed teens—who courageously reached out and obtained help, showing that there is a better way. Combining the skill of a medical professional and the compassion of a family member touched by the reality of depression and the unnecessary tragedy of suicide, Bev has carefully gathered research about what depressed teens and family members can do. She has coupled this lifesaving information with the inspiring stories of teens who came forward to share their experiences of depression, despair, and eventual recovery.

This volume, just like Angey, Amber, David, Cera, Paul, Heidi, Shaneeka, Heather, MacKenzie, Shawnelle, and Tyler, who tell their stories within its pages, breaks down the walls of silence and stigma, piercing the myth of misinformation. The medical information is top-notch and up-to-date, and the stories are touching and true.

Suicide is an unnecessary tragedy. Yet, given its frequency among youth, only such courageous and candid steps forward to share much needed medical information and alternative role models will allow us to change the end of the story for youth like Kurt Cobain. This volume is a major step forward.

Peter S. Jensen, M.D.
Ruane Professor of Child Psychiatry & Director
Center for the Advancement of Children's Mental Health
Columbia University, New York City

Introduction

"Sometimes I feel I can't go on. My life's not worth it; I don't belong." —Sydney, 14

Maybe you feel the same way sometimes—sad, discouraged, alone, and tired. These feelings may seem scary, confusing, and overwhelming, especially if you think you're the only one feeling them. This book can help you see that many other teens—perhaps some of your friends, classmates, neighbors, or team members—might be going through the same thing you are. I want you to know that your life *is* worth it. You *can* go on.

I wrote the original edition of *When Nothing Matters Anymore* a decade ago, after losing three family members to suicide. Their lives were full of turmoil and emotional anguish at the time of their deaths. The most recent of the suicides was that of my cousin, Kurt Cobain, the lead singer of the rock band Nirvana, who shot himself on April 8, 1994. I know something about what they felt because I have dealt with my own depression since I was a teen, and I have experienced being suicidal.

After Kurt's death, I spoke with teens, reporters, and well-wishers. Many people asked me why someone with such wealth and fame would kill himself, why Kurt was so "selfish," and why he didn't think about his wife and child and the pain his death would cause them. Nobody asked the most important questions: *What problems was Kurt facing that seemed too huge to solve? What could someone have done to help him?*

I read what the media had to say about his suicide. Newspapers, magazines, and TV reporters commented on Kurt's heroin and alcohol use, his "angst," and his inability to cope with success. These weren't the problem—they were symptoms of the problem. Kurt suffered from bipolar disorder* (also known as manic depression), a mood disorder affecting about 2.3 million people in the United States alone. Kurt's untreated depression was part of what caused the emotional

---

*For more information about bipolar disorder, see pages 24–27.

and physical pain he so desperately needed to escape. Killing himself seemed, to Kurt, like the only way to be free of the pain he could no longer bear.

I've heard some people say that suicide is a stupid, weak, and shameful act. What they don't know is that suicide is a cry for help. Few people outside of the mental health field understand depressive disorders, how they often relate to suicide and drug/alcohol problems, and how common these issues are among teens. I hope this book will continue to shed light on the terrible toll that depression takes on young people.

Since the first edition of this book was published, much has changed in what is known about depression—and yet, much has stayed the same. I believe that, as a society, we have moved a step forward in the acceptance of depression as a serious issue among teens and adults. Experts recognize that depression can start as early as childhood and, left untreated, often continues into adulthood. People are now more willing to talk about depression and to share their feelings and fears with family members, doctors, therapists, and school counselors. In addition, there is a greater awareness of medications as part of the treatment for depression, and perhaps less stigma about their use. Knowledge like this is a powerful tool—it helps us to better understand depressive disorders and what to do about them.

What hasn't changed as much as it should is that many teens *aren't* getting the help they need. A survey released by the Substance Abuse and Mental Health Services Administration in 2005 showed that about 2.2 million adolescents (ages twelve to seventeen) had experienced at least one major depressive episode in the previous year. Less than half received treatment during that time. The survey also revealed that the depressed teens were more than twice as likely to use illegal drugs as their peers. According to the National Youth Violence Prevention Resource Center, more than 90 percent of teen suicide victims suffer depression or drug/alcohol abuse. It is my hope that this book will help depressed teens find a light in the darkness—perhaps it will even save lives.

When Nothing Matters Anymore is divided into two parts. Part 1, "What's Wrong?" explores how it feels to be depressed, the causes and types of depression, and the connections between depression, suicide, and drug and alcohol abuse. Part 2, "Getting Help and Staying Well," discusses the benefits of professional treatment and how to help yourself stay healthy. If you think you might be depressed or suicidal, or if you're abusing drugs and/or alcohol, the best thing you can do to help yourself is to talk to an adult you trust. It may be difficult to open up to someone, share your problems, or ask for help, so throughout Parts 1 and 2, I've provided suggestions for what you can say. You'll find "You Can Say" sections on pages 30, 58, 75, 81, 115, and 116. At the end of each chapter, you'll also find a Survival Tip that can help you right now, during treatment, and for the rest of your life—so you can live well and reduce the possibility of getting depressed again.

This book wouldn't have been possible without the help of many courageous young people who allowed me a very personal glimpse into their lives to share what depression was like for them: what happens, what hurts, what's hidden, what haunts, and what helps. I hope reading their stories will help you see that you aren't alone.

Feel free to write to me with your questions, thoughts, and comments. You can send your mail to:

Bev Cobain
c/o Free Spirit Publishing Inc.
217 Fifth Avenue North, Suite 200
Minneapolis, MN 55401-1299

Or email me at: help4kids@freespirit.com

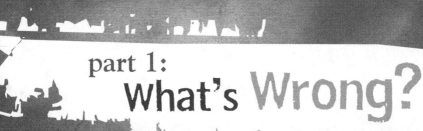

part 1:
What's Wrong?

"*Most problems precisely defined
are already partially solved.*" —Harry Lorayne

"It's like a gray cloud descends over me from nowhere."
—Cera, 18

Depression: The Facts

Everyone feels down in the dumps, bummed out, or sad at times. If nobody had these normal feelings, there wouldn't be music called "the blues." People would feel cheerful even after flunking a test, losing a ballgame, or breaking up with a girlfriend or boyfriend. Being in a bad mood for a few days is natural. Gloomy, unhappy feelings are part of life, and they usually pass.

But sometimes the mood hangs on, affecting your emotions, your body, your behavior, your thoughts. Maybe you're unable to get out of bed and face the day. It's like you've fallen into a deep, dark hole with no way to climb out. Experts call this mental state *depression*.

Did you know that:
- an A student can be depressed?
- a star athlete can be depressed?
- someone who's handsome or beautiful can be depressed?
- a change in appetite can signal depression?
- a sudden drop in your grades or trouble in school could be a sign of depression?

- if you're often angry and irritable, you might be depressed?
- when you feel like nothing matters anymore, you're probably depressed?

Depression causes a variety of serious symptoms and can affect anyone at any time—no matter who you are or where you live. People young or old can be depressed. People of any race, gender, ethnic heritage, and religion can be depressed. Even teens who are healthy and cope pretty well with their problems can experience depression.

Famous People with Depression*

Abraham Lincoln, sixteenth U.S. president

Alanis Morissette, Canadian singer, musician

Ann-Margret, actress, entertainer

Audrey Hepburn, actress

Axl Rose, rock singer

Barbara Bush, former first lady

Ben Stiller, comedian, actor

Betty Ford, former first lady

Billy Joel, singer, musician

Boris Yeltsin, former Russian president

Brooke Shields, actress

Carrie Fisher, actress, novelist

Charles Darwin, British naturalist

Charles Dickens, English novelist

Claude Monet, French impressionist painter

Darryl Strawberry, baseball player

Delta Burke, actress

Diana, Princess of Wales (Lady Di)

Dick Clark, entertainer

DMX, rapper, actor

Drew Barrymore, actress

Edgar Allan Poe, poet, short story writer

Edwin "Buzz" Aldrin, astronaut

Elton John, British singer, musician

Emily Dickinson, poet

Eric Clapton, British singer, musician

Ernest Hemingway, novelist, short story writer

Eugene O'Neill, playwright

Florence Nightingale, British nursing pioneer

George Stephanopoulos, political adviser

George Washington, first U.S. President

Georgia O'Keeffe, painter

Hans Christian Andersen, Danish fairy tale writer

Howard Hughes, aviator, industrialist

Jane Pauley, broadcast journalist

Jean-Claude Van Damme, Belgian martial artist, actor

Jim Carrey, comedian, actor

John Milton, English poet

Judy Garland, singer, actress

Kay Redfield Jamison, psychiatrist, writer

Larry King, broadcaster, talk show host

Leo Tolstoy, Russian novelist

Louie Anderson, comedian

Ludwig van Beethoven, German composer

Margot Kidder, actress

Marie Osmond, singer

Marilyn Monroe, actress

Marlon Brando, actor

Mary Chapin Carpenter, country singer, songwriter

Menachem Begin, sixth prime minister of Israel

Michelangelo, Italian Renaissance artist

Mike Wallace, broadcast journalist

Norman Rockwell, painter

Oksana Baiul, Ukrainian figure skater

Patricia Cornwell, crime novelist

Patty Duke, actress

Queen Elizabeth I of England

Ray Charles, R&B singer, musician

Richard Nixon, thirty-seventh U.S. president

Robert E. Lee, U.S. general

Robin Williams, comedian, actor

Roseanne Barr, comedian, actress

Sheryl Crow, singer, musician

Sigmund Freud, Austrian "father of psychoanalysis"

Sir Isaac Newton, English mathematician, physicist

Stan Collymore, English footballer

Stephen Fry, English comedian

Sting, English singer, musician

Sylvia Plath, poet

Ted Turner, media mogul, philanthropist

Tennessee Williams, playwright

Terry Bradshaw, football player

Theodore Roosevelt, twenty-sixth U.S. president

Thomas Jefferson, third U.S. president

Tipper Gore, wife of U.S. vice president Al Gore

Trent Reznor, singer, musician

Vincent van Gogh, Dutch painter

Virginia Woolf, British novelist

Vivien Leigh, English actress

William Blake, British poet, painter

Winona Ryder, actress

Winston Churchill, English politician, author

William Styron, novelist

*Some people listed here are celebrities who have spoken openly about their depression. Others, especially historical figures, are recognized as having signs and symptoms of depression.[1]

According to the National Institute of Mental Health (NIMH), about 18 million Americans currently are depressed, and millions of them are teens. If you are feeling down, guilty, worthless, angry, overwhelmed, helpless, hopeless, tired, and/or anxious—and if these feelings have affected you for some time—you're probably depressed.

Depression Q & A

Is it my fault I'm depressed? **No**

Does being depressed mean I'm weak? **NO!**

Does being depressed mean I'm crazy? **Of course not!**

Can I get well again? ***Absolutely!***

Depression is a medical illness. That means it's not "all in your head." It isn't a sign of weakness, a punishment for past wrongs, or a flaw in your character or personality. Depression also is a *treatable* medical illness—that means it's possible to deal with it and heal.

On the following page is a quiz that can help you figure out if you have symptoms of major depression, the most common form of depression.* The questions will help you learn more about your feelings and behavior.

If you think you might be depressed, talk to someone. You can tell a parent, a teacher, a school counselor, or another trusted adult. If you need to know how to tell someone you're depressed, see the suggestions on pages 30–31.

---

*For more information about major depression, see pages 20–21.

How to Tell If You Might Be Depressed (a Quiz)

If you answer yes to four or more of these questions, and you've had symptoms almost continuously for two or more weeks, you might have major depression.

	Yes	No
1. I often feel sad and anxious.	☐	☐
2. I feel worthless and/or guilty.	☐	☐
3. I'm easily irritated.	☐	☐
4. My appetite has changed drastically.	☐	☐
5. I don't enjoy things I used to like to do.	☐	☐
6. I have little or no energy.	☐	☐
7. I sleep too little or too much.	☐	☐
8. I have trouble concentrating/making decisions.	☐	☐
9. I have violent outbursts/trouble with self-control.	☐	☐
10. Some people think I'm loud and obnoxious.	☐	☐
11. I skip school or have dropped school activities.	☐	☐
12. I often have headaches or other aches.	☐	☐
13. I use alcohol or illegal drugs to help me feel better.	☐	☐
14. I feel hopeless about the future.	☐	☐
15. I feel helpless to change my situation.	☐	☐
16. I think about death, suicide, or harming myself.*	☐	☐

*If you answered yes to this question, please talk to someone right away. Confide in an adult you trust or call a Crisis Hotline or Suicide Hotline listed in your Yellow Pages. You may also call the Girls and Boys Town National Hotline 24 hours a day at 1-800-448-3000 (a trained professional will respond).

A Word About Depression in Teens

Teen depression is a confusing illness because many of its symptoms are like the normal (but uncomfortable) feelings associated with puberty and growing up. When you're a teen, your hormones—chemicals in your brain and bloodstream—increase and change your body chemistry. You may sometimes feel moody, negative, emotional, and stressed out. This is normal and usually temporary. Symptoms of clinical depression, however, last for more than two weeks.

Teens often identify their depression themselves, instead of a parent or teacher noticing it. Why? Because sometimes it's hard for parents and other adults to know whether your feelings are a normal part of being a teen or are symptoms of a more serious problem. So it's important for you to be aware of changes in your moods and behaviors. To figure out if you might be depressed, watch for extreme changes in the way you feel, think, and act—these changes are intense and painful, and they affect you for more than just a few days.

Emotional changes:

- anger
- sadness
- guilt
- hopelessness
- anxiety
- bitterness
- irritability
- feeling worthless
- indifference
- feeling numb
- loneliness
- feeling helpless

Physical changes:

- sleeping problems (too much or too little sleep)
- overeating or loss of appetite (with weight gain or loss)
- indigestion
- headaches
- nausea
- aches and pains for no known reason
- fatigue, lack of energy, or no motivation

Thinking changes:

- difficulty remembering or concentrating
- difficulty making decisions
- confusion
- a loss of interest in things you used to enjoy
- self-blame for anything that goes wrong
- pessimism (negative thinking)
- believing no one cares about you
- believing you're a burden to others
- believing you don't deserve to be happy
- thoughts racing through your head
- thoughts of harming yourself*
- thoughts about death and suicide*

Behavior changes:

- poor hygiene
- aggression
- talking or moving with much more or less energy
- acting out (skipping school, running away, driving too fast, trying risky sexual behaviors)
- extreme sensitivity to rejection or failure
- problems at school
- abusing drugs and/or alcohol
- spending most of your time alone (isolating)
- not participating in class or with family and friends (withdrawing)
- being unable to relax
- crying more than usual
- underachieving (or overachieving)
- harming your body (like cutting or burning yourself)*

*If you're thinking about suicide, please talk to an adult you trust right away. You can also call a Crisis Hotline or Suicide Hotline listed in your Yellow Pages.

Remember that you're looking for changes/symptoms that have lasted for two weeks or more. If you've had many of these symptoms for months or years, you may not even realize they were changes.

"For some reason, people don't realize that boys have hurt feelings, too. I have had sadness since I was a small boy. What helped me were my friends, my music, and finally my parents talking me into seeing a counselor. It has made a really big difference to have someone I trust to talk to when my feelings start to bother me." —James, 14

Try recording your feelings, thoughts, and behaviors in a journal for a few days or a week or two—whatever you can handle. Having a written record may help you see a pattern. Share your writings with a trusted adult who can help you find out if you're depressed. Here are some ideas to help you get started:

Feelings Journal

Emotionally, I feel . . .

Physically, I feel . . .

Some things that are hard to deal with are . . .

Sometimes I worry about . . .

I feel better when . . .

I think I could talk to . . .

The Good News

There's good news?!

If knowing you're depressed makes you even *more* depressed, take heart because:

1. Depression is common.
2. It's treatable.
3. You don't have to face this alone.

Many depressed people mistakenly think they're crazy or dying of a terminal illness. They're actually relieved to know they're depressed. You may feel less scared and more hopeful once you know the reason for your symptoms. With help, you can stop suffering; life doesn't have to be so full of pain. Isn't it somewhat of a relief to know that you don't have to feel this way any longer?

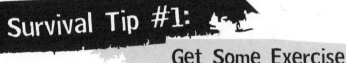

Survival Tip #1:
Get Some Exercise

When you're depressed, you might feel sluggish, achy, tired, and run-down. You may not want to leave the house, get out of bed, or get off the couch. One way to help yourself while you're recovering from depression is to exercise. Even if it seems impossible, do something physical. Exercise helps defeat depression.

Experts have found that exercise affects chemicals in your brain (and brain chemicals have a lot to do with depression). Exercise releases chemicals called *endorphins*, giving you a natural high. Endorphins lift your mood, energize you, and may help you sleep more soundly at night. The more often you exercise, the better you'll feel.

Even moderate exercise can have positive effects. In fact, researchers at the University of Texas at Austin conducted a study in 2006, proving that 30 minutes of brisk walking could temporarily boost the mood of depressed people.[2] The researchers pointed out that many depressed people self-medicate with alcohol, illegal drugs, or nicotine to temporarily change the way they feel or to get through their day. However, walking—an activity with no lasting negative health consequences—can be a mood-lifter that actually works. You don't need any special gear for walking, and it can be done just about anywhere. Try to keep going for half an hour—you will probably see a difference.

If you feel too tired to exercise, tell yourself that you can do something for just five minutes; after that, you may have the energy to keep going for a few more minutes. Try some jumping jacks, hop on your bike, or put on a CD and dance. Eventually, work your way up to doing 20 to 30 minutes of continuous exercise several times per week, which will help keep your level of endorphins more constant. Be sure to vary your workout routine so you don't get bored, and don't try to push yourself too hard.

Yoga is another option—a gentle, noncompetitive form of exercise that can help strengthen your body and soothe your mind. The word "yoga" means union (referring to the joining of the physical, emotional, and spiritual elements of life). The slow, rhythmic stretching movements lead to greater balance, reduced stress, and an improved ability to concentrate or relax fully—all of which can help you feel better both physically and emotionally. You might find a class at your community center or YMCA/YWCA, or borrow a DVD from the library to learn the poses. Once you've learned the basic poses, you can create your own routine to a piece of music that moves you. You can do yoga with a friend or on your own.

If you have trouble getting motivated to do any type of physical activity, ask a friend or family member to be your exercise partner. Make plans to work out together a few times a week, even for a short time. Go on walks together and take along your dog (or a neighbor's dog). It's been proven that spending time with a pet can reduce stress and anxiety, and lift people's moods.

You might want to keep an exercise journal, so you have a record of what you've accomplished and how you feel.

Exercise Journal

Today I exercised by . . .

I spent this much time exercising . . .

Afterward, I felt . . .

Sports/activities I'd like to try . . .

Ways to reward myself for taking good care of my body . . .

Ideas for staying motivated . . .

People who can help me . . .

"It was my stepdad who realized
I might be depressed. He listened to me
and got help for me. He's awesome."
—Kevin, 13

Types of Depression

Nestor is sixteen and lives in Costa Rica. He's the youngest in his family, with four sisters and a brother. Nestor's family owns a bar/restaurant in a small village and also raises cows and pigs. He has a large extended family of aunts, uncles, and cousins.

Even when surrounded by his loved ones, Nestor felt lonely. He has a lisp, and since childhood, the other kids have laughed at him and teased him for it. Because of the teasing, Nestor spoke only as much as necessary and was afraid to meet new people. He so disliked going to school that he dropped out after sixth grade.

By the time Nestor was fourteen, he had already been sneaking *guaro,* an alcoholic drink made from sugarcane, from his family's bar for about four years. Nestor then started using illegal drugs because he felt that he could better tolerate his fear and loneliness when he was high. But combining drugs and *guaro* quickly changed Nestor. He became angry and belligerent toward his parents and relatives. He stayed away from home for days at a time, telling his parents that he was staying at the home of one of his sisters. Nestor would cry over nothing. He slept most of the day and went out at night. Sometimes, he slept around the clock. He lost weight and refused to help his family with chores.

Nestor's family realized that his behaviors were more than just typical teen troubles, but they didn't know what to do. They sent him to live with one of his married sisters—they thought she could "talk some sense into him" and keep him off drugs. Nestor tried to comply with his sister's rules, and he even went to talk to a priest. But neither the priest nor Nestor's family members knew much about the effects of drug withdrawal or depression. At last, one of his uncles realized the extent of Nestor's problems and recommended a drug rehabilitation center in San José, a six-hour bus ride away.

Nestor was to stay at the center for a month. There, he met with a psychiatrist who diagnosed Nestor's major depression and drug addiction. The doctor prescribed an antidepressant, talk therapy, and daily Alcoholics Anonymous (AA) meetings. But again, Nestor was lonely. Unlike many of the other patients, he had no visitors. His family was far away. After two weeks, he ran away from the center and hitchhiked home.

When he got there, he learned that his oldest sister had given birth to a baby boy, whom she named Nestor. The family called him Nestorito (Little Nestor). Nestor went to see his namesake and instantly fell in love with him. He stayed with him, holding him whenever possible and helping his sister with the baby's care. She informed Nestor that she wouldn't allow him near the baby, unless he was completely sober and gave up the drugs. She encouraged him to take his prescribed medication and continue with the AA meetings at least three times a week.

This time, Nestor stuck with his treatment. He moved in with his sister and the baby, and is now helping to raise his nephew. Nestor has learned to value himself as an uncle and more importantly as a person, which has given him the courage to go on.

How can someone feel lonely and lost within their own family, like Nestor did? And how can the signs of serious problems—like depression and addiction—go unchecked for so long? The reason is that depression can be difficult to recognize. The signs of it aren't always obvious to other people or to the person who's depressed. Depression isn't like the flu, where the symptoms appear suddenly and are hard to mistake. Depressed people can feel awful for weeks, months, or even years before understanding that something is seriously wrong.

There are many different kinds of depression, too: melancholia, reactive depression, Seasonal Affective Disorder (SAD), and postpartum depression, to name a few. If you ever feel like reading the *Oxford Psychiatric Dictionary*, you'll find up to twenty-five types of depression; they vary in the number of symptoms and how severe they are.

Teens are most likely to experience:
- major depression
- dysthymia (pronounced dis-THIGH-mee-a) or
- bipolar disorder

Major Depression

Major depression (also known as clinical depression) is the most widespread type—you might even call it the common cold of brain illnesses. If you're a girl, you may be more prone to major depression because of the physical and hormonal changes of puberty, especially if you're struggling with identity problems and a drop in your self-esteem. In fact, studies have shown that although boys and girls have about the same rate of major depression during childhood, at age fourteen, suddenly twice as many girls as boys suffer from major depression.

The quiz on page 11 can help you spot the signs of major depression.

Watch for symptoms like these:
- feeling sad, empty, guilty, anxious, worthless, irritated, and/or hopeless
- feeling tired, fatigued, or slowed down
- a loss of interest in activities, hobbies, and/or relationships
- interrupted sleep or oversleeping

- trouble concentrating, remembering things, and making decisions
- a change in appetite (with unintentional weight gain or loss)
- restlessness
- violent outbursts and obnoxious behavior
- use of alcohol or drugs to try to feel better
- physical symptoms (headaches, pain, digestive problems) that won't go away
- thoughts of suicide or death, or suicide attempts*

*If you're thinking about suicide, please talk to an adult you trust right away. You can also call a Crisis Hotline or Suicide Hotline listed in your Yellow Pages.

Major depression isn't something you can grow out of, and it usually won't go away on its own. Untreated major depression can last for a year or two—or more. Your symptoms might bother you for a long time, making it hard to keep up in school, have fun with your friends, get along with your family, and enjoy life.

If you think you might have major depression, talk to someone about it. Maybe you're too depressed to share your feelings with anyone, or maybe you have doubts about asking for help. Getting help *works*. It's worth it, and so are you.

Angey's Story

Angey's symptoms of depression began during the summer before sixth grade. Around that same time, she swallowed several pills from the medicine cabinet and had to be hospitalized. Her dad didn't realize what Angey had done, and she didn't tell the doctors what she had taken, so no one knew what she was really going through. Soon after, she began cutting as a way to cope with her pain. Cutting is a form of self-injury or self-harm, which some people use as a way to punish themselves, express inner

pain, feel a sense of control in their lives, or distract themselves from intense emotions.

I started sixth grade still feeling a little sick from the pills I took and still depressed. My friends thought I was getting too strange, so I started hanging out with a different crowd. I felt ashamed, guilty, and worthless, and I thought no one cared for me. I felt like the world hated me. For the next few years, I cut and took any pill that would make me feel "good."

When I was in seventh grade, two of my best friends killed themselves. I was horrified and felt like I wanted to die, too. It's all I could think about. Around this time, I went to a concert of the band Good Charlotte. During the concert, the band talked about how much people really mean to them, how much people truly love us, and how suicide is not the answer. I broke down and cried. At that one moment in my life, I felt I belonged—that someone cared.

Good Charlotte is my favorite band. My love for their music helped me want to stop behaving in destructive ways. Their music made such a huge difference in the way I think and feel about myself. Depression is difficult, and I needed help to get better—but I made it.

I have seen several therapists and finally found one who is awesome. He talks to me like I'm a person, instead of a child. He listens to me and tells me what he thinks. He doesn't act as if he knows more than I know about myself. I am someone to him.

I also found that an antidepressant has helped me a lot. In fact, I feel so much better that I recently wrote about my experiences in a speech, which I read in front of the student body of my school. As a result of doing that, I was asked to volunteer for a youth outreach program that helps teens like me every day. My grades are much better now, I actually like school, and I have my friends back. It isn't easy. I still have to watch myself and my thoughts, but I'm doing it.

"There is hope for a happy life. Look for help. Sometimes you have to fight for it. Don't give up." —Angey

Dysthymia

Dysthymia, also called dysthymic disorder, causes many of the same symptoms as major depression but in a milder form. It's a "low-grade" depression (kind of like a low-grade fever), where you start living life almost as if you're going in slow motion. When you have dysthymia, you're usually able to carry out your daily routines, but it may take a lot of effort for you to do things that other people seem to do easily.

Dysthymia is chronic—it goes on and on. In fact, teens usually have dysthymia for a minimum of a year.

If you have dysthymia, you might feel:

- unloved
- sad
- angry or irritable
- hopeless
- guilty

- self-critical
- negative
- bored
- tired
- anxious

You might also:

- have trouble concentrating or making decisions
- experience a sudden drop in your grades
- sleep too much or too little
- act out or become disobedient (lie to your parents, misbehave at school, cheat on tests, shoplift, drive under the influence, etc.)
- have aches and pains with no apparent cause
- think about suicide or death, or attempt suicide*

*If you're thinking about suicide, please talk to an adult you trust right away. You can also call a Crisis Hotline or Suicide Hotline listed in your Yellow Pages.

Because dysthymia can lead to major depression, it's important to get help as early as possible. Talk to an adult about your situation before it gets worse. You *don't* have to live with chronic sadness and fatigue—you can experience all the joy and excitement the world has to offer.

What's SAD?

You may have heard the term "SAD," which stands for Seasonal Affective Disorder. It's a kind of depression that occurs only during fall and winter, when the days get shorter and it gets dark earlier. If you have SAD, you may feel sluggish, irritable, and anxious. You might also binge eat (especially carbohydrates like bread and pasta), then gain weight. Come spring, your dreary mood will probably lift and you'll feel more energetic. Experts believe that the pineal gland, a small structure located near the center of the brain, plays a role in SAD. The pineal gland is activated by light. Many people who suffer from SAD have been able to relieve their symptoms through exposure to a special artificial light for 30 minutes or more each morning and evening.

"My mom thought I was lazy because I was tired and bored most of time. We found out I have dysthymia during a health checkup, and after getting treatment, I feel like a different person." —Josh, 15

Bipolar Disorder

Bipolar disorder, also known as manic depression, involves episodes of major depression and "mania." Although professionals call bipolar disorder a mental illness, you're *not* crazy or insane if you have it.

"Bipolar" means your moods go back and forth between two (bi) opposite (polar) emotional states. When you're depressed, you may feel sad and hopeless. When you're manic, you may be extremely angry, irritable, or happy; have extraordinary mental and physical energy; and have boundless confidence. Your mood might swing from overly high and irritable (during the manic phase) to low and hopeless, then back to manic again.

Bipolar disorder is difficult to recognize and diagnose in children and teens because the symptoms may be different than what is typically seen in adults. For example, adults may experience longer periods of mania or depression (lasting for months), while kids and teens can bounce back and forth between these moods every week or in a single day. In addition, bipolar disorder affects each individual in a particular way; your signs and symptoms could be quite different from the next person's. And because the symptoms may also be seen in other conditions such as Attention Deficit Hyperactivity Disorder (ADHD), anxiety disorders, conduct disorder, or substance abuse, it takes an expert to determine what may really be going on with you. That expert will need to observe your behavior over a period of time and have information about your health history in order to provide an accurate diagnosis.

If you think you might have bipolar disorder, take a look at the quiz on page 11 , which can help you find out if you have symptoms of major depression. With bipolar disorder, you'll have those symptoms some of the time and manic symptoms at other times. You may feel like you're riding a roller coaster of highs and lows.

The symptoms of mania (a manic episode) include:

- feelings of exceptionally high energy, happiness, and creativity
- extreme irritability
- a tendency to be easily distracted
- a decreased need for sleep
- racing thoughts and hyper-alertness
- increased moving and talking
- grandiose ideas, overconfidence, and/or a feeling of being invincible

- difficulty making decisions
- obnoxious behavior
- denial that there's a problem
- risk-taking behaviors, including drug/alcohol abuse

Bipolar disorder tends to run in families and may be inherited, but just because someone in your family has the illness doesn't mean you'll get it. Children under twelve have been diagnosed with bipolar disorder, but it often starts in adolescence or early adulthood (and continues throughout life). The number of teen boys and girls with bipolar disorder is the about the same.

Bipolar II disorder is a milder form of the illness, which causes "hypomania," or periods where you suddenly feel energized, more friendly, less shy, intensely interested in things, and even powerful, sensual, and euphoric. If you think this mood feels "good," you might deny that anything's wrong. But the mood isn't normal. You may soon be very moody, irritable, or reckless, and you'll eventually sink into a depression.

Many people don't realize that they have bipolar disorder and struggle needlessly for a long time. Dr. Rich Adler, a Seattle psychiatrist who works with teens, explains it this way: "What young people need to know about the disorder is that very early in the illness—in the early teens—there may not be obvious mania or clear depression. Instead, they may be irritable, agitated, or aggressive without knowing why. Hyperactivity is the hallmark of bipolar disorder." It's easy to misread the signs of bipolar disorder. You and your family (even your doctor) may have assumed that something else is causing your moods and behavior. Sometimes, you have to see more than one expert to find the help you need.

Bipolar Disorder Resources

An Unquiet Mind: A Memoir of Moods and Madness by Kay Redfield Jamison, Ph.D. (Alfred A. Knopf, 1995). Jamison, a psychiatrist, has struggled with bipolar disorder since adolescence—this book is her personal testimony of how the illness shaped her life.

Bipolar Disorder for Dummies by Dr. Candida Fink and Joe Kraynak (For Dummies/John Wiley & Sons, Inc., 2005). If you like the "For Dummies" books and want to understand some basics of bipolar disorder and its treatment, this resource can be helpful. The book addresses not only the person with "BP" but also family and friends, who are often affected by the moods and behaviors of their loved one.

Mind Race: A Firsthand Account of One Teenager's Experience with Bipolar Disorder by Patrick E. Jamieson, with Moira A. Rynn, M.D. (Oxford University Press, 2006). Part of the "Adolescent Mental Health Initiative" series, this personal account of a bipolar teen's experiences also includes information about treatment options and tips on coping at home and at school.

Amber's Story

Amber's experience with bipolar disorder began for certain when she was eight years old, but probably earlier. Her story shows how difficult it can be to diagnose the illness and how hard bipolar disorder can be on family members.

AMBER, AGE 15: I've always had angry outbursts. As a toddler, when I had temper tantrums, I banged my head against the wall and screamed. My mom didn't realize at the time how serious this was. As I got older, my anger worsened.

By the time I was twelve, I felt angry all the time. I broke things. No matter what anyone said to me, I took it personally and went into a rage. I said things just to make my mom feel bad; when we walked down the street together, I'd say, "Why don't you just jump in front of that truck?" I didn't know why my life felt so awful. I hated my mom because I thought she didn't understand me. I believed that my feelings and actions were her fault. I would think, "Why can't I be different? Why do I act and feel so hateful?" Sleep was nearly impossible for me. I'd dance, sing, and write poetry all night, then go to school in the morning.

By the time I was thirteen, I was into alcohol and illegal drugs. I ran away, got arrested, and was always in trouble. I stayed away from home for weeks at a time. I had a twenty-one-year-old boyfriend. I knew I was doing bad things, but I never considered the consequences.

Two days before my fourteenth birthday, I went to juvenile detention. I was there for two weeks, and I did a lot of thinking. I felt that I had dug myself into a hole and was spiraling downward, faster and faster. I was skinny and strung out. My friends were disappearing because they had no way to predict when my moods would change.

My mom thought I had a chemical imbalance in my brain, and I began to wonder if she might be right. I saw a doctor who realized I have bipolar disorder, and I was put on lithium.*

I didn't change overnight, but gradually I started feeling different. I still felt like me—Amber—but better. I stopped flying into rages. I still got angry, but I could talk about it now. I still felt happy sometimes, and I still felt sad sometimes. Instead of always feeling crazy, I just lived.

> **"Maybe you happened to be born with bipolar disorder. It doesn't mean you're a bad person. Getting help can be like starting a new life."**
> —Amber

My brain isn't chaotic anymore. I can sit and have a calm conversation, and I'm in control of my thoughts. I see a counselor to talk about my problems, and I'm learning about morals, consequences, and boundaries. I'm also learning to deal with the things I ran from my whole life. I have fun now, I laugh, and I go to sleep at night like other people.

---

*For more information about lithium and other medications for bipolar disorder, see pages 102–104.

AMBER'S MOM: When Amber was younger, she cried a lot and threw things, but I thought she was just a pretty little girl with a mind of her own. It never occurred to me then that something might be wrong. She would go for days with no sleep at all or for weeks with only a few hours of sleep a night. While everyone else slept, she was awake, writing and dancing. When she started running away for weeks at a time, I'd look at what she'd written and cry. Some of it made no sense at all.

She got mad about everything. If I acted silly, she got mad. If I got mad, *she* got mad. If I told her I liked something about her, she'd say I was lying. I tried not to laugh, joke, or talk around her. I thought about how horrible it must be for her to feel so miserable. Seeing her hurt herself really hurt me. When she would run away, I'd be out looking for her at midnight, banging on the doors of her friends' homes. Sometimes I'd find her and bring her home, but she'd just run off again. She told me she was taking drugs to "feel the way everybody else felt." I couldn't hang on to her and couldn't get through to her. I was watching my daughter destroy herself, and I felt helpless, frustrated, and angry. I refused to give up on her, though.

Taking medication was hard for Amber in the beginning, but today it's working. We occasionally argue, but if either of us starts yelling, I just leave the room for 20 minutes to calm down. When I return, Amber has calmed down, too, and we hug. We need that little break. One day not long ago, Amber turned to me and said, "Mom, I love you. I want you around when I get married and have children." And I said, "Amber, haven't we come a long way? Not so long ago you told me to throw myself in front of a moving vehicle." We laughed about it together. We've discovered that Amber has a wonderful sense of humor that had been strangled all those years by her illness.

Last summer, Amber worked at a camp for autistic and developmentally disabled children. She was so patient with them and grew to love even those who struck her or bit her. Amber reminds me not to believe that she's perfect now, but I trust her because she's finally able to think of consequences and to consider the feelings of others. I finally have my daughter back.

Okay, I'm Depressed. Now What?

Talk to an adult you trust. Reach out to your parents, if you feel comfortable talking to them; they may not realize that you're depressed, especially if you've been hiding your feelings. If you're hesitant to confide in a parent, ask yourself why.

Are you scared that he or she:
- doesn't care about you?
- won't listen to what you say?
- will judge you?
- won't understand your feelings?

Maybe you're afraid to admit your feelings to the adults in your family. Although it can be scary to talk about feelings, the adults who love you will listen and will probably do what they can to help you. Getting things out in the open may be a relief, so give your parents a chance to understand what you're going through. If talking to a parent isn't an option, go to another adult family member, a teacher, a religious leader, your school counselor, a school social worker, your principal, a coach, a mentor, or another adult you trust.

You Can Say:

- "I'm feeling awful, and I think I might be depressed."
- "I'm feeling so down that I don't care about anything anymore. I guess I'm going to need some help."
- "I don't like the way I've been acting lately. I feel so angry (sad, helpless, scared). Maybe I need to see a doctor."
- "I know my grades are slipping, but I don't seem to care about school anymore. I need to do something to feel better."
- "I'm tired (grouchy, irritable, anxious) all the time. I think I might be depressed. Will you help me decide what to do?"
- "I need to tell someone how sad and confused I feel."
- "Nothing feels 'right' with me anymore. I wish someone would help me."

Sometimes it's easier to start this kind of a conversation by asking a question.

You Can Ask:

- "Have you ever thought no one cared about you, but you weren't sure why?"
- "Have you ever felt sad and afraid, like you might be depressed or crazy?"
- "Did someone ever break up with you and you thought you'd never be happy again?"
- "Have you ever felt really guilty about something and had a hard time talking about it?"
- "Have you ever felt like nothing matters? Like everything is falling apart?"

Survival Tip #2: Take a Break

"Rest is not a matter of doing absolutely nothing. Rest is repair."
—Daniel W. Josselyn

Depression can make you feel tired, so take it easy on yourself. It's okay to rest when you need to. Taking time to relax is a way to clear your mind, recharge your batteries, and restore your health. Get used to taking a break from your activities and allowing yourself to rest for 15 to 30 minutes every few hours during the day.

Ways to relax:
- take a nap
- soak in the bathtub or a hot tub
- read for pleasure (not a homework assignment)

- call a friend
- breathe deeply and slowly (see the relaxation exercise on pages 32–33)
- pet your cat or dog
- massage your feet
- listen to your favorite relaxing music (no sad songs)
- daydream
- doodle
- lay on the grass and watch the clouds go by
- tell yourself positive things like "I can feel better"

A Relaxation Exercise*

A relaxation or deep-breathing exercise can help you cope with stress, focus your thinking, and relax your body and mind. You'll feel calmer, and with practice, this type of exercise will become easy and natural. Here's how to do it:

1. Pick a spot where you won't be disturbed and get comfortable.
Lie on your back. If you feel like you're going to fall asleep, sit up so you don't become *too* relaxed.

2. Relax and become aware of your breathing.
Feel your breath moving in and out of your body. Get a sense of where one breath ends and another begins. Next, pay attention to any unwanted tension in your body. Sometimes you don't even realize that the tension is there until you're lying still. Common hiding places for excess muscle tension include your forehead and facial muscles, neck and shoulders, chest, lower back, and your hands and feet.

---

*This relaxation exercise is adapted from *The Right Moves to Getting Fit & Feeling Great!* by Tina Schwager, P.T.A., A.T.,C., and Michele Schuerger (Free Spirit Publishing Inc., 1998), pp. 39–40. Used with permission.

To help yourself relax, perform the following sequence, beginning at your head and slowly working your way down your body.

- Tense your forehead, jaw, and cheek muscles. Hold for a count of five. Take a deep breath, and as you exhale, let those muscles relax. Envision all your stress draining away.

- Squeeze your shoulder blades together and tighten your chest. Count to five, take a deep breath, and as you exhale, relax your muscles and all the tension within them.

- Lock your elbows, clench your fists, and push your arms against the ground. Hold for a count of five. Take a deep breath, and as you exhale, let your arms go limp.

- Now squeeze your rear end and your stomach muscles. Hold, count to five, inhale, and as you exhale, slowly relax your muscles.

- Move the focus to your legs. Flex your thighs, push your knees down, pull your toes back toward your shins, and dig your heels into the floor. Keep tightening these muscles. Hold for a count of five. Take a deep breath, and as you exhale, let go of all the tension in your muscles.

- Lie still and notice any remaining tension you may feel anywhere in your body. Take a deep breath, and as you exhale, imagine the rest of your tension pouring out of your body, into the floor, through the earth, and disappearing forever.

Relaxing is a skill that takes some time to get used to, so be patient with yourself. Enjoy the soothing feelings that deep breathing can create.

"I'm glad to say that I'm getting better. I'm back to my writing and other hobbies. I am so full of hope. I have my sad times, my hard times, but now I have this feeling in the back of my mind that tells me that things will get better and that I just have to take a deep breath and think. *I can make it better.*" —Amanda, 12

"One morning, I woke up and no matter how hard I tried, I couldn't stop crying."
—Danielle, 18

How Depression Affects Your Brain

Depression affects your brain, which leads to mental, emotional, and even physical changes (so you might think of depression as a "whole body" or "whole being" illness). Your brain is your body's most complex organ; it's much more intricate than the most sophisticated computers. It transmits and receives information through electrical messages passed along your body's nerve pathways. Your brain produces and uses special chemicals called *neurotransmitters* to move these messages along the nerve cells. In fact, your brain sends *billions* of messages each second to all areas of your body with one goal: to keep you alive and healthy.

Mouth! Yawn. Stomach! Growl for food. Eyelids! Heavy, need sleep.

Your brain produces and stores many neurotransmitter chemicals, but three main ones have been studied in connection with depression.

These chemicals are:
- norepinephrine (NOR-ep-uh-NEHF-run)
- dopamine (DOHP-uh-meen) and
- serotonin (SEHR-uh-TOH-nun)

These three chemicals move messages to and from your brain along specialized nerve cells (called *neurons*) throughout your body's central nervous system. Your neurons are unique and don't look exactly like anyone else's, but they have the same basic parts, including *axons* and *dendrites*. When your brain sends a message, it travels as an electrical signal along the axon of a neuron. Between the end of one nerve cell and the beginning of another is a tiny gap known as a *synapse*.

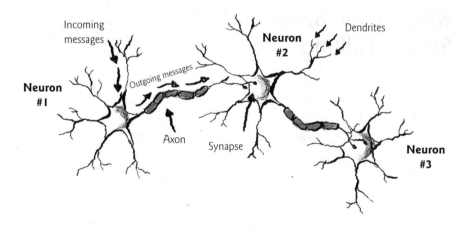

The message needs to cross the synaptic gap, so the transmitting cell releases one of its chemicals (for example, serotonin). The molecules of serotonin fill the gap and attach themselves to the next cell, forming a "bridge of serotonin." The message travels across the gap, is processed by the next neuron, and continues along that cell's axon to the next gap, where more serotonin is released. This process continues until the message reaches its destination. Once the message is delivered, the serotonin has done its job and is no longer needed; it's then reabsorbed by the transmitting cell (a process called *reuptake*). If you don't have enough serotonin available for release into the synaptic gap, millions of messages aren't properly transmitted to the receiving cell. The disruption leads to symptoms of depression.

Imagine that the "depressed" brain is a large company (say, the Acme Rug Company) with all sorts of important functions and responsibilities. Now pretend that the company has a disabled communications center—all the different departments must try to communicate with each other over frayed and disconnected telephone wires, short-circuited lines, and cords plugged into the wrong places. What happens? The departments can't communicate or get anything done. If you're depressed, your brain (like the imaginary Acme Rug Company) can't communicate properly—important messages to your body are simply lost in transmission.

When Your Brain and Body Stop "Talking"

Why does depression affect your brain, body, moods, and behavior—everything about you? Because when you're depressed, your brain and body can't work together well enough to help you function normally. Your body depends on your brain to tell it to eat, drink, sleep, move, and feel. When your brain and body stop "talking," you're unable to process these important messages (it's like your brain is giving you the silent treatment).

Your brain's limbic system helps regulate your emotions and

I just don't feel like talking.

your motivation. It's made up of several different areas, each responsible for certain tasks. Here are some examples:

- The **thalamus** screens and sorts messages from your senses (sight, smell, touch, hearing, and taste). If your thalamus doesn't receive the messages correctly, one result might be that foods don't look, smell, or taste appealing.

- The **hypothalamus** is the source of your feelings, including your sexual feelings; it also controls your blood pressure and tells you when you're hungry and thirsty. If your hypothalamus is impaired, you may feel hungry a lot, lose your appetite, or have an increased (or decreased) interest in sex.

- The **amygdala** can activate anger and aggression or make you feel calm, depending on the part that's stimulated. Overstimulation or understimulation of the amygdala may cause problems with anger and self-control.

- The **hippocampus** forms and stores new memories. If your hippocampus isn't working properly, you may have trouble learning new things or remembering what you've learned.

- The **Reticular Activating System (RAS)** alerts your brain that messages are coming from the five senses, then helps you concentrate by filtering this input. If this function fails, it may be hard for you to focus. The RAS also is responsible for regulating sleep (sleep disturbances are the number one complaint of depressed people).

- The **cerebellum** is responsible for posture, balance, and muscle coordination. If messages aren't transmitted properly in this area, you might have difficulty playing sports or just doing normal daily activities.

- The **cerebrum**, the largest part of your brain, does the "thinking" jobs like solving problems, making decisions, and receiving, storing, and retrieving memories. Your intellect, language skills, and ability to understand numbers and the alphabet are all based in your cerebrum. If the nerve cells in your cerebrum aren't functioning well, you may not be able to think clearly, use good judgment, or communicate effectively with other people.

In fact, when you're depressed, normal functions like eating, sleeping, walking, thinking, feeling, and remembering may seem like monumental tasks.

Causes of Depression

Experts have different opinions about what causes depression. Many believe, for example, that depression is a result of chemical imbalances in the brain. Other experts say that your genes, environment, or coping skills play a big role in whether you get depressed. Most likely, depression is the result of a combination of factors.

What Your Body and Genes Have to Do with Depression

Hormones, like neurotransmitters, carry messages between your nerve cells and your brain. Your hormones are responsible for transporting information that affects the growth and development of your body. If you're depressed, you might have abnormal hormone levels—specifically, levels of the hormone cortisol, which is produced in response to stress or fear.

If you're a girl, you're probably familiar with PMS (premenstrual syndrome), which can happen when your hormone levels are higher during the week before your period. The excess hormones might make you feel irritable, anxious, emotional, and out of control—depressed, in other words. Girls and women who have given birth have high hormone levels afterward, and this can lead to a form of depression known as postpartum depression.

Other physical conditions can contribute to depression, too. For example, if you have an eating disorder (such as anorexia nervosa, bulimia, or compulsive eating disorder), you're more prone to depression. If you have a chronic illness—diabetes, epilepsy, arthritis, asthma, etc.—you may be dealing with physical and emotional symptoms that are painful and hard to manage, which can lead to depression.

If you've been diagnosed with depression before (a "prior episode"), you may be more likely to get it again. According to Dr. Boris Birmaher, a psychiatrist at the University of Pittsburgh Medical Center,

"Each episode of depression may change some biological mechanism in the brain and trigger more depressions. This is referred to as 'the kindling phenomenon.'" Just as kindling helps start and spread a fire, a prior episode of depression can spark future depressions.

The genes your parents passed to you can play a part in whether you're at risk for depression. Studies have shown that relatives of people with depression are two to three times more likely to suffer from it themselves. In other words, you may inherit a genetic vulnerability. But just because you have a genetic risk doesn't automatically mean you'll become depressed.

Other risk factors for depression include:

- **a "perceived difference,"** such as obesity, a physical disability, a learning disability, or homosexuality. Because you may seem and feel different, you might have a low self-image or be teased by others, which can contribute to depression.

- **anxiety disorders,** such as excessive worrying, obsessive-compulsive disorder, or panic disorder. These problems can increase your risk of depression, and they may even make your symptoms more severe and long-lasting.

- **conduct problems** like temper tantrums, shoplifting, or skipping school. If acting out is a result of depression and you're punished for your behavior, you may feel guilty, angry, or worthless—this can increase your depression.

- **being gifted and talented.** You might assume that you have "enough smarts" to handle any emotional difficulties, so you might hold in your feelings instead of talking about them. Anyone—gifted or not—can suffer from depression. It's okay to admit that you have a problem and need help.

"My depression began a few years ago, when I was eight or nine. I got depressed because kids at school called me names like 'Cow,' 'Chubs,' and 'Blowfish.' It hurt so bad that some days I wanted to die to make the pain go away." —Andrea, 11

David's Story

Nineteen-year-old David has been diagnosed with major depression. His grandfather on his mom's side had depression, and David's great uncle has bipolar disorder. Because David has a weight problem, he's been teased and mistreated by the other kids at school all his life. From elementary school through high school, he felt extremely anxious about going to class and dealing with the other students. Extreme anxiety may lead to depression.

I'm six feet and one inch tall, and I weigh about three hundred pounds. Being large runs in my family. I have a brother who's thin, but my older sister and my parents are all large. Our love for each other is also large. We respect and care for each other more than any other family I know. I've never had a reason to doubt my family's love for me. The parents of every one of my friends have divorced, but my parents have been married for twenty-six years. I sound like I should be a fairly happy and secure guy, don't I? Up until recently, nothing could be further from reality.

By third grade, I had been called every name you can imagine because of my weight. I made up any excuse to avoid going to school, where I was humiliated, taunted, and regularly beaten up. I was never a fighter. I learned kindness and compassion from my parents. The teachers tried to help me, but they couldn't protect me all the time. I grew severely anxious. I'd do whatever it took to stay home. I pretended not to wake up, feigned illness, and even learned to make myself throw up. I clung to my bed and cried. I became so afraid of going to school that even when no one bullied me, I was filled with panic.

I began seeing a therapist while I was in fourth grade, and I came to think of him as my friend. I liked going to see him, but it didn't make my fear go away. I missed many school days on and off for the next couple of years. In middle school, I had such terrible anxiety that I cried all the way to school each day. I pretty much stayed in the library all the time. I was escaping instead of learning to cope.

I only stayed in that school for half a quarter, then I transferred to another middle school. I sat in the back of each class, so frightened that all I could do was shake and cry. I did the same thing through most of seventh and eighth grades. I was so impaired by anxiety that my attendance was very poor. I couldn't tell anyone what I was afraid of because I didn't know. No matter how hard I tried, I couldn't control the fear. By this time, my doctor had diagnosed my problem as agoraphobia, which means fear of open places. Many people with agoraphobia are afraid to leave their homes, but I was just afraid to go to school.

When I started high school, I had to interact with older kids, and I was even more scared. I told my parents that I intended to drop out of school. I realized that not finishing high school could negatively impact my life, but I was in serious pain. My parents were against my dropping out, but in the end, I had to make my own decision. Soon after dropping out, I scheduled an appointment with a psychiatrist for an in-depth evaluation of my anxiety and feelings of helplessness. I continued to see this doctor, and within two months, he was able to establish that I suffered from a chemical imbalance in my brain. He thought I had major depression, and he prescribed medication, which ended up helping.

"If you get down, take things as they come. From my own experience, I know the pain will subside. If you need to talk to someone, you can talk to your friends and family."
—David

Today I'm the same nice, large guy that I've always been—minus the tears, anxiety, and depression. I've been attending an alternative school for three years now, and I'll graduate this year. I've taken up scuba diving with my dad, and I enjoy it a great deal. It's the only real exercise I get, but it's a workout. I usually go on Fridays and feel great for the rest of the week. Life goes on: I still have to deal with things just like everyone else does, but now I don't struggle under the shadow of depression.

Cera's Story

Eighteen-year-old Cera was a senior at a progressive private school when this interview took place. She may have inherited a risk for depression from her mother, who has dealt with depression herself, but Cera also has another risk factor: She's a lesbian.

I was always "the difficult child." I don't think it really had much to do with my sexuality, but my family and I were constantly at odds. Our personalities seemed to be completely incompatible, and my parents seemed to look for a scapegoat for our problems (I was often it). I had to find different people to confide in.

I relied a lot on my friends for support. I always have, and I assume I always will. But when you're gay and you look around and can't see anyone else your age like you, it's scary—terrifying, in fact.

I had transferred from many schools, trying to find a place where the kids were interested in changing the world. I ended up at a progressive alternative school that I liked. But I had too much to deal with—a combination of confusion about my sexuality, enduring a sexual assault, and terrible family conditions. I had too much to cope with, and I was depressed. Suicide was an option I considered often.

I was unique in my coming out because I didn't wait to tell my family and friends until I was secure in a gay identity. It was more like, when I knew, *they* knew. My parents reacted by saying, "It's a phase. You've always tried to be different, and this is just another way."

My school proved invaluable in keeping me grounded. For the first time, I was in almost daily contact with gay adults, and I also had the ability to explore numerous options on the Internet. Chat rooms were priceless to me during that confusing period of my life. They were anonymous, which meant I could be gay, depressed, and me, and not get stressed about being judged.

Most of my close friends knew about my lesbianism. I was terribly lucky that they stuck by me. Somehow though, just having my close friends know wasn't enough for me. I made a decision—I wanted to tell my entire school. I wanted to prove a point. Gay adults were okay at my school, but there weren't any "out" students.

I came out during a Martin Luther King Day assembly, where we were identifying groups of people who were having their rights denied for some reason. I stood before them, reading from a list I had made of several women, their jobs, their relationships, and their interests. As I neared the bottom of my list, I mentioned my own relationships and interests. Then I said that all these women had one thing in common: They were lesbians. It was funny—quite a few people didn't pick up on the message. Many people already knew I was a lesbian, or had guessed. The response to what I considered a huge declaration, however, was overwhelmingly positive.

Depression is still a daily part of my life. I still haven't found any therapy or medication that has been completely effective, so I rely on my art and my friends to pull me through. My parents have gotten a lot better about my sexuality; it hasn't been an issue for a couple of years now.

"Hang in there. There *are* resources; there *are* people who care and can help, even if they don't know you. Find them. Use the Internet. Keep the hope." —Cera

My mother goes to PFLAG (PFLAG stands for Parents, Families and Friends of Lesbians and Gays) meetings with me, and last year she was the "F" in the Pride Parade for PFLAG. My father occasionally attends the meetings, too. I have a big online PFLAG family that I'm still in touch with.

I think role models are so important for other gay teens. The Internet supplied a lot of those role models for me. It can be a dangerous medium because of some of the creeps who hang out there, but the Internet is also perfect for self-exploration because of the anonymity it provides. The list of Web sites for gay teens is growing hourly. PFLAG has a ton of resources. There's definitely support out there; sometimes you just have to search for it a little bit harder.

The world is beginning to realize that gay teens and depressed teens exist. I think the only way to keep on reminding them of our existence is to speak up and find the resources we need.

Gay and Lesbian Resources

GLBTQ: The Survival Guide for Queer & Questioning Teens by Kelly Huegel (Free Spirit Publishing Inc., 2003). This comprehensive handbook offers expert insights, true stories, helpful advice, and more. The author, who works with PFLAG (Parents, Families and Friends of Lesbians and Gays), includes her personal account of growing up confused and different, and shares how a suicide attempt led her to seek the support she needed.

Lambda Legal Defense and Education Fund
120 Wall Street, Suite 1500
New York, NY 10005
(212) 809-8585
www.lambdalegal.org
Lambda Legal works to help protect the civil liberties of GLBTQ (gay, lesbian, bisexual, transgender, and questioning) people.

OutProud—The National Coalition for Gay, Lesbian, Bisexual, and Transgender Youth
369 Third Street, Suite B-362
San Rafael, CA 94901
www.outproud.org
This information-packed Web site includes news, coming out stories, discussion groups, online brochures, links to other sites, and a community role models archive.

Parents, Families and Friends of Lesbians and Gays (PFLAG)
1726 M Street NW, Suite 400
Washington, DC 20036
(202) 467-8180
www.pflag.org
PFLAG provides materials and support for GLBTQ teens and their families. The Web site includes information about their programs, such as the safe schools campaign, as well as electronic versions of many of PFLAG's pamphlets.

Note: Stay safe as you surf by making sure you always know who sponsors a Web site, who's giving advice on a bulletin board, and what type of information is okay to share about yourself when chatting online. You can never be sure about who you're talking to online, so be careful and make good decisions. Don't give out personal information such as your phone number or address. Be wary of anyone who requests a photo immediately or who asks to meet with you in person alone. Meeting someone you've become acquainted with online could be risky. To be on the safe side, bring along a parent, a guardian, or another trusted adult.

What Your Environment Has to Do with Depression

Experts believe there's a connection between "stressors" (things that cause stress) and teen depression. Although stressors don't necessarily cause depression, they may *trigger* it, especially if you have other risk factors for the illness. Environmental stressors occur outside you—within your home, school, or community. Examples of stressors include divorce, peer pressure, sexual or physical abuse, violence, and poverty.

The stressors may be out of your control, but you *can* learn to control how you react to them. Say, for example, that you flunk an important test at school. How do you react? Do you (A) feel disappointed for a few days, get support from a parent or friend, then recover and move on? Or (B) feel like a total failure, keep your disappointment to yourself, and become overwhelmed by your painful feelings? If you chose A, you probably have good coping skills and a network of friends and family members who offer support when you need it. Your coping skills can help protect you from depression.

But what if you chose B? You may have a poor opinion of yourself and difficulty coping with painful events. Maybe you don't think your family, friends, and teachers are supportive—maybe there's no one you feel comfortable talking to. If this sounds like you, you could be at risk for depression. Holding your feelings inside—especially anger, sadness, and disappointment—can make you feel like you have no control over your life or what happens to you. When you feel powerless to change your life, you're more likely to become depressed.

Other stressors include:

- a drop in your self-esteem
- family conflict (especially if it's frequent)
- financial problems (your own or your family's)
- the letdown after achieving a goal (a feeling of "Now what?")
- any unwelcome change in your life (including the onset of puberty)
- physical, mental, or sexual abuse (current or past) *

*If you're in an abusive family situation, or if you've been abused in the past, talk to an adult you trust. A parent, a school counselor, a doctor, a religious leader, or another trusted adult may be able to help. If that's not comfortable for you, look in your Yellow Pages for the number of a Crisis Hotline.

What do all these events have in common? A sense of loss. Whether it's the loss of feelings of security, family harmony, or pride in yourself, you may feel like your life has changed for the worse. No matter how good your coping skills are, this kind of grief can affect you profoundly, and you may feel you have nowhere to turn. Maybe your parents or other family members don't know how to deal with emotional issues themselves and aren't offering you much support.

Family troubles often trigger or worsen depression. If you're a depressed teen living in a home where there's conflict or abuse, you'll probably have more episodes of depression than other teens. If your family is troubled, you may feel like you can't express your emotions or concerns, or that you lack support. You may feel you're at the mercy of your environment and are helpless to change things.

It's scary to reach the limit of what you can handle. You may feel that no one understands you or cares about you—or has ever felt the same way you do. When you reach this point, you may not know how to cope anymore. If you use negative coping behaviors, like numbing yourself with drugs and/or alcohol,* your depression will only worsen. If you withdraw from family and friends, you're putting more of a burden on yourself because you're shutting out people who might be able to help you.

The best things you can do for yourself:
1. Admit you need help.
2. Reach out and trust someone.

If you don't have a supportive family, finding a trusted adult may be difficult, but not impossible. You can talk to a teacher, your principal, your school counselor, your school social worker, a religious leader, or a family friend. Give yourself permission to cry, get angry, or be afraid—this helps you release your feelings and puts you in a better position to deal with them.

Take a look at what's going on in your life right now:
- Have you experienced a loss recently?
- Do you lack a network of people you can turn to for support?
- Are you suffering from a sense of low self-worth?
- Do you have a family history of depressive illness or abuse?

Once you're aware of your risk factors, you can begin to understand the reasons behind your depression. It's not your fault if you're depressed—it's no one's fault. You didn't ask to have depression, but if you do, you need to ask for help. Your mind and body need—and deserve—to get better.

The Biggest Loss
Everyone has experienced grief in their lives. Grief is a natural response to losing someone or something you love—such as when a parent leaves, a close friend moves away, or a romantic relationship ends.

---

*For more information about drugs and alcohol, see Chapter 4.

Feelings of pain, confusion, disbelief, and sadness follow. These feelings intensify if the loss was due to the death of a loved one, because this kind of loss is forever.

The death of a beloved family member or a pet are events that cause profound grief that can last for weeks, months, or years. Typically, a grieving person goes through five stages, which vary in how long they last. The five stages of grief aren't written in stone—some people skip stages or experience them in a different order.

The five stages of grief:
- **Denial**—you don't believe the death happened, or you pretend it didn't and that your life can go on normally.
- **Anger**—you feel anger or rage that the person you love has left you behind.
- **Bargaining**—you start to believe that if you change your behavior in a certain way or do the right things, the person you love will return.
- **Depression**—you feel deeply sad, helpless, and alone.
- **Acceptance**—very gradually, you begin to accept the loss and take steps to get on with your life.

Losing a loved one to suicide can be even more difficult to handle. Because the death was intentional, the survivors (those left behind) are stunned and often believe that they should have seen it coming or could have done more to prevent it. The emotions involved in being a survivor are terribly complex. In addition to the usual stages of grief, the survivor often feels intense guilt and a sense that there is very little support (because of the stigma that surrounds suicide).

A suicide occurs at least every seventeen seconds in the United States, and every three seconds worldwide. So it's likely that you or someone you know has experienced this type of grief. Lynette DePeer, a therapeutic clinician who helps teens in this situation, knows first-hand what being a survivor of suicide feels like. Her life was irrevocably changed by the suicide of her father when she was fourteen. According to Lynette: "I was destroyed by my father's suicide. How could I not have known he was in such pain? Determined not to let others see how fragile and desperate I was, I pushed myself into school and sports activities. No one knew I was crying in the morning while I was getting ready for school, in the locker room, and after dinner in my room. I was on the honor roll, but I was a mess."

During the grieving process, many teens turn to drugs, alcohol, or sex as a temporary release from the pain they're feeling. Lynette has seen teens who use these counter-productive measures to mask their true feelings and fill the sad and empty places inside themselves. She herself experimented as a teen, which she says only added to the shame she was already struggling with. Lynette's mom, worried about her young daughter's continuing grief, located a Survivors of Suicide (SOS) group, where Lynette was encouraged to talk about her feelings with people who truly understood. "The SOS group provided the tools and support I needed to navigate my grief process. I couldn't bluff. These people knew what I was going through. I was able to say whatever I wanted and needed to say with unconditional support. I actually gained a respect for my grief and my process—a lesson I find extremely useful in my work with clients today."

Survivors' Resources

Dying to Be Free: A Healing Guide for Families After a Suicide by Beverly Cobain and Jean Larch (Hazelden, 2006). The suicide of a loved one leads to deep feelings of guilt, confusion, fear, and grief—leaving the survivors (family members, relatives, friends) desperate for answers. This book offers personal accounts of the aftermath of suicide, as well as advice on coping with grief.

Survivors of Suicide
www.survivorsofsuicide.com
The purpose of the Survivors of Suicide Web site is to help those who have lost a loved one to suicide resolve their grief and pain in their own personal way. Although geared mainly toward adult survivors, the site includes helpful information, FAQs, links, support, and more.

For more information on suicide, including resources, see Chapter 5.

If you're sad, angry, anxious, or depressed, ask yourself if you may be feeling grief over a loss you've experienced. Even something that happened long ago could still be causing you pain. Talking about your feelings with an adult or within a support group will help you express your grief, deal with difficult emotions, and move forward on the path toward acceptance and healing.

Paul's Story

Paul's first depression occurred at age seven, when his parents divorced, and it lasted for about two years. After seeing a child psychiatrist, Paul began to feel better. When he was twelve, he went to a school where he felt left out, discouraged, and alone. Nirvana, one of Paul's favorite bands, sang about the kind of isolation Paul was feeling. When Kurt Cobain committed suicide, Paul experienced this as a profound personal loss, which led to another depression.

I live in Cape Town, South Africa, where there are two cultures—English and Afrikaans. I'm English. At age twelve, I went to a conservative bilingual school with mostly Afrikaners. I felt "apart" from the others because I came from a different background. I liked a totally different type of music than most of my classmates, spoke a different language, and thought their parties were sort of "square." There were different cliques in the school, and I didn't feel like I fit in with any of them. Some of the Afrikaners didn't like me. I played water polo and studied classical piano, so I didn't quite get along with the jocks. I felt left out and misunderstood.

I think this is why Nirvana's music appealed to me so much. I thought that Kurt Cobain had experienced the same sort of "separateness" that I felt, since it was the core of his music. Even though our living circumstances and family lives were very different, I thought there was a strong similarity in the way Kurt and I felt about things. Listening to Nirvana's music comforted me and helped me let out my anguish. I got so attached to the music that, in a way, I was living in it.

When Kurt died, I fell into an extremely depressed state. I felt very, very, very alone. I didn't want to see anyone. I didn't speak. I tried to think, but I was confused. My thoughts went in circles, and nothing made sense. Something I loved had suddenly been taken from me, and I wondered how I could go on without it. How could this loss fit into my life?

I think some kinds of depression are triggered by your circumstances. For me, Kurt's death was a great enough loss to make me depressed again. I lost interest in everything; sometimes I wouldn't even leave my room. I didn't want to go anywhere or do anything, not even get out of bed and walk around the house. For the first time, Kurt's music didn't comfort me.

I tried to write about all the things I felt, but at the worst stage, I couldn't identify my feelings. I had no words to describe them. Later, when I could write a little, capturing some of my feelings on paper helped. I wrote a long piece about Kurt's life, making little drawings and adding some of my thoughts.

I was very depressed for several weeks. When I finally returned to school, I still had the same "lost" feelings, but to a lesser degree. People at school didn't really know what was going on with me, and I didn't want to talk to anyone about it. This was a really sad point in my life. Now, when I think back to that time, there's shame—a sort of "What were you thinking?" kind of shame. I couldn't see ahead—it was like being in a time capsule. Now it's all in the past, and at the moment I don't have a problem with depression.

"I'm happy with my circumstances. You can be, too. It's possible to get beyond your depression and have a better life." —Paul

Survival Tip #3:

Have Some Fun

"Laughter is the shortest distance between two people."
—Victor Borge

Laughter makes you feel good. Research has shown that laughter increases your breathing rate, muscular activity, heart rate, and other body functions. When you laugh, you feel better and happier—it's a good way to temporarily relieve some of the symptoms of depression and to keep your spirits up while you're recovering.

When you're depressed, you might isolate yourself from your friends, family, and other people who care about you. Isolation makes you feel more sad and lonely, increasing your depression. One thing you can do as you start to feel better is spend time with a friend doing something fun. Go see a funny movie or rent a funny video or DVD, go to a live comedy show, or just listen to a recording of your favorite comedian.

If you've been isolated for a while, you may feel a little awkward about suddenly being social, but renewing and initiating friendships can help you fight depression. Take it slowly at first, if you need to.

If you're grieving the loss of a loved one, that pain is very real—but so is your need to reach out to others, laugh, and have fun. It's not a betrayal of the person you lost to go out and do things you used to enjoy. You can still ride your bike or board, go to the park or mall, express yourself creatively, laugh, make others laugh, and talk to people. Stay busy. Stay connected.

Ways to be social:

- attend a sporting event or a musical performance at school or in your community
- have a party and invite close friends and people you'd like to know better
- get a football, basketball, or volleyball game going with your neighbors
- invite a friend or neighbor for dinner
- join a club or get involved in a new activity at school
- email or write a letter to a relative or friend

Other ways to feel good:

- buy yourself a present (it doesn't have to be expensive)
- write down five positive things about yourself (if you can't think of any, ask a family member to help you come up with a few)
- read a funny book, a cartoon collection, or a humor magazine
- read the Sunday comics and cut out cartoons that make you laugh
- buy a joke book and memorize some jokes to share

"Until my mom took me to a counselor, I felt so alone and overwhelmed. With help, I have finally begun sorting out my feelings. I think everything will be all right." —Danielle, 19

Drugs, Alcohol, and Depression

Being a teen isn't an easy job. It seems like everyone has expectations of you—your friends, parents, teachers, relatives, and employers. Sometimes you may think your life is out of control. Your body is changing rapidly, and you may be worried about your looks, your emerging sexual feelings, and what other people think of you. On top of all that, you probably have schoolwork, family issues, a job, and sports or other activities to handle—all these pressures can leave you feeling overwhelmed and stressed out.

The one person who generally has the highest expectations of you may be *you*. Guess who usually has the least confidence in you? That's right, *you*. It's normal to feel shaky about growing up, how your life is changing, and what the future holds. You may wonder if you're as good looking, smart, cool, or talented as other people; you may be hiding your true self because you think people won't like the real you.

If, on top of everything else, you're also depressed, life becomes even more difficult. It may help a little to know that *nobody* goes through life without hurting some of the time. No matter how good-looking, intelligent, successful, or popular you are, you'll still feel pain.

That's the way life is: We lose people or pets we love, we go through breakups, and we hurt others or make mistakes. Why? Because we're human, and life isn't perfect.

How do you cope when your life feels out of control? Maybe you wish something would make you feel good—like you think everyone else feels. Or maybe you're looking for comfort. If you reach for drugs and/or alcohol to feel "better" or to numb your pain, the toxic chemicals become a way to hide from reality. Drugs and alcohol can't help you cope with your pain, make you feel better, or put you back in control of your life. Only *you* can do these things.

A Little Known Fact

Many teens have major depression an average of *four and a half years* before turning to alcohol and/or drugs to deal with their pain.[3] The good news is there's a window of opportunity for your parents, teachers, and other adults in your life to help you deal with your depression *before* you turn to drugs and alcohol for comfort. Depression affects lots of people—it's okay to admit it and ask for help (it shows you care about yourself). Getting help—whether it's for depression, drug and alcohol abuse, or both—is a step toward getting better.

What Happens When You Abuse Drugs and Alcohol?

If you're depressed, you're probably in a lot of emotional pain—you may feel sad, helpless, and angry. It's also possible to feel emotionally numb or "dead" inside. What happens if you try to soothe or medicate yourself with illegal drugs or alcohol? Drugs (pot, cocaine, speed, hallucinogens, crack, heroin, etc.) and alcohol (beer, wine, or hard liquor) make you feel different, but not necessarily better. You may get high or drunk and *temporarily* anesthetize your feelings, but eventually the effects of the chemicals wear off and you're back where you started. You might believe that the chemicals can help you find comfort, escape your pain, and feel more alive, but when you put harmful substances in your body, you're giving up control of yourself and your life—the chemicals take over.

If you decide to abuse alcohol or other drugs, you're hurting yourself. (Notice I use the word "abuse," not "use"; I don't think that, as a teen, you can *use* alcohol and/or drugs without *abusing* yourself.) Drug and alcohol abuse makes your life much worse. You can't control any part of your life if you're letting something else control you.

Abusing drugs and/or alcohol can:

- cause symptoms of depression
- mimic depression
- trigger depression
- worsen depression
- mask the symptoms of depression

If, for example, you abuse cocaine, amphetamines, or inhalants, you may be irritable, have racing thoughts, or have trouble sleeping or functioning. The manic phase of bipolar disorder* can cause the same symptoms. An expert trying to determine what's wrong with you might not know for sure whether you have bipolar disorder or a drug problem—or both.

---

*For more information about bipolar disorder, see pages 24–27.

If you abuse alcohol or drugs like Valium, barbiturates (Pheno-barbital), steroids, prescription painkillers, or heroin, you might have mood swings, fatigue, and difficulty concentrating or remembering. People with major depression or dysthymia* also have these symptoms. Hallucinogens like LSD and Ecstasy can make you react in different ways, depending on your mood, your environment, and how much of the drug you take. You may act manic (a symptom of bipolar disorder) or feel sad, scared, angry, and anxious (symptoms of depression).

The Risk of Meth

Crystal Meth is the synthetic, crystalline powder form of amphetamines; basically, it's a deadly form of speed cooked up with a mix of medications and solvents. The drug (also known as crystal, tina, crank, rock, and ice) is so potent that some experts think it's impossible *not* to get addicted to it—once it takes hold it won't let go. Meth acts by changing how your brain works. Whether inhaled, snorted, or injected, the drug ends up in the blood circulating through your body, damaging— sometimes permanently—thousands of neurotransmitters in your brain.

If someone you know is using meth, you may not be able to stop him or her, but you can help by talking about the risks, getting an adult involved, and/or by calling a Crisis Hotline to find a drug treatment center in your area. If you need help yourself, see the list of resources on pages 67–68. It can be scary to ask for help, but your life depends on it.

Maybe you've tried to escape your painful feelings by using marijuana or alcohol. These drugs aren't "mild" or "harmless." Pot can have a sedative effect (making you feel sleepy), or it may cause a "psychedelic" experience, where you hear and see things much differently than usual—either way, you're worsening your symptoms of depression. You'll probably feel tired and have problems concentrating, and if

---

*For more information about major depression, see pages 20–21. For more about dysthymia, see pages 23–24.

you smoke pot every day, you may feel continually fatigued, depressed, and anxious, and have trouble remembering.

Alcohol is dangerous, too, because it's a depressant—it slows down your central nervous system and may intensify your sadness and lack of energy. In other words, marijuana or alcohol might lift your mood or dull your pain for a very short time, but the crash that follows can leave you lower than you were before. Alcohol is particularly dangerous for teens because it can damage a part of your brain that isn't fully developed until adulthood. According to Traci Toomey, an epidemiologist at the University of Minnesota's School of Public Health, getting drunk also puts you at a very high risk for alcohol poisoning, injuries, and sexual assault. Another disturbing fact: Teens who drive while drinking are twice as likely as those twenty-one and over to be involved in fatal accidents.[4]

"I've been incarcerated for quite a long time because of some bad decisions I made, including drinking and driving. I was a very angry kid and caused my parents a lot of problems. We have learned to talk things out since I've been here, and I will be leaving for my home soon, with a much better attitude and with ideas to keep myself from becoming depressed again." —Jeremy, 16

To get help for a drug and/or alcohol problem, find an adult you trust. Following are some ways to talk about what you're going through.

You Can Say:

- "I use pot (beer, wine, hard liquor) once in a while. I want to stop, but I'm worried I'll feel down (sad, angry, scared) all the time. Can you tell me how to get help?"

- "I'm afraid to tell my parents that I've been using drugs (alcohol) as a way to numb myself. I can't seem to handle my feelings, and I'm wondering if you can help me."
- "I'd like to quit using drugs (alcohol), but I don't want to lose my friends who are using. What should I do?"
- "I'm doing drugs, and I want to stop. What can I do?"
- "I know drugs (alcohol) are messing me up, but I hate the way I feel most of the time. Do you have any ideas for me?"

Heidi's Story

Sixteen-year-old Heidi, who has epilepsy, had a history of family problems and depression. She put herself in many risky situations, abusing drugs and alcohol and having unprotected sex. As a result, Heidi got pregnant at age four-teen and had an abortion. Although she went through a lot, she eventually found a coun-selor who could help her with her problems.

When I started middle school, I was living with my dad and was very depressed. So many things had happened to me. I wasn't getting along with my mom and stepdad, and I had recently been diagnosed with epilepsy. On top of all that, something terrible occurred right after moving in with my dad: I was raped by a man who followed me home. I felt very angry, dirty, confused, and sad. I lost all my self-esteem.

I couldn't get along with my dad—he knew nothing about raising a daughter. He didn't approve of my friends, which led to awful fights, and when he was at work, I just did what I wanted. The battles wors-ened, and my dad placed me in a group home, where he thought I'd be better supervised. I hated it there. I promised my mom that I would fol-low her rules if she'd let me live with her, and she let me come home.

Before long, I met an older guy who paid lots of attention to me. He was nineteen, but I told my mom and my stepdad that he was sixteen. My mom didn't even want me to talk on the phone with this guy—she didn't realize that I snuck out at night to see him.

My boyfriend never gave me flowers or other gifts, but he did give me alcohol, and that made me feel special at the time. I thought, "Wow, an older guy wants me to drink with him!" To me, it was a big deal. I never thought about the consequences of drinking, and I didn't even consider refusing the alcohol. I wanted my boyfriend to think well of me. We also did drugs together. I smoked pot, but I was never really into it; I didn't like feeling as if I had no control over my body. Sometimes I skipped school to use marijuana.

My boyfriend and I began to have sex, and he never used a condom. He told me he couldn't get me pregnant, so I foolishly assumed he was sterile. I knew absolutely nothing about birth control. When I missed two periods and started getting sick in the morning, I realized I was pregnant. I asked my boyfriend to help me pay for an abortion, and he said the pregnancy wasn't his fault. I was crushed. He just blew me off, and that really hurt.

A few days after my fourteenth birthday, my mom and I were arguing. I told her I was pregnant because it was easier to tell her while I was angry than while I was feeling afraid. A part of me wanted to keep the baby, but I realized I had no way to take care of it. I had an abortion, and for the first month or two afterward, I didn't think I was that affected by it. Then one morning, I woke up thinking about the abortion, and I couldn't believe what I'd done. I was horrified. I thought, "My God, I've killed a baby!" Everything slowed down so I could think, and the force of my realization was overwhelming.

Six months after the abortion, I was deeply depressed, and things continued to get worse. I started to see a twenty-one-year-old man, and when my mom and stepdad found out, they got really upset. When they took the phone away from me one night, I became enraged and smashed things in the house. My mom called the police, who took me to temporary foster care until our family could sort things out.

A local mental health agency got involved and provided a counselor for me. My counselor, Sol, was the best thing that ever happened to me. I finally had someone who would listen to my feelings. At one session, I mentioned to Sol how badly I needed a job so I'd have my own money. She told me about a job at the Center for Wooden Boats, where kids were involved in a boat-building project that would

> **"My mind is opening more each day. I've learned that the choices you make determine how your life will go."** —Heidi

take six weeks and pay each person $690. I thought the idea of building a boat was kind of corny, but it was a way to make money. Two weeks later, I was at orientation at the Center, along with a group of other kids.

During the project, we all lived in a group home. We were told that the boat-building experience would challenge our ability to work in a highly structured environment. That day, I started the project with a bunch of strangers, a blueprint, some wood, and a lot of skepticism. We were supposed to build an *umiak*—a type of boat made of sealskins and whale bones by the native people of the Arctic. The boat would be twenty-six feet long. Each new day, I was given a specific task. I worked hard for long hours; it felt fantastic to step back and see what I'd accomplished as part of a team.

Over the next six weeks of instructions, laughter, tears, frustration, and wonder, a beautiful boat arose amidst the scraps and dust—an amazing boat that when lifted by twenty-five helpers and workmates and set gently into the water, miraculously floated! I became aware of a second miracle that day: *I felt wonderful.* I felt magnificent. I felt good about myself for what seemed like the first time in my life. I wondered how I could have gone the whole six weeks without noticing how I was changing. I think that the whole time I was doing my part to build a strong new boat, I was also building a stronger, more confident me. When I was given the honor of writing the blessing for the boat, I felt very proud.

Abuse vs. Addiction

What's the difference between *abusing* drugs and alcohol and being *addicted*? When you abuse chemicals, your use of them interferes with your health and your ability to function at home, at school, on the job, and in social situations. For example, you might binge on the weekends, which means you get out of control and take risks that you might not ordinarily take. But when you're addicted to alcohol and drugs, you have a *physical need* for the chemicals your body craves. You can't go without them and will do almost anything to get them.

If you're abusing, you might:

- have trouble going to school and work, keeping up with your activities, or getting along with your family
- have problems in your relationships
- put yourself in physically dangerous situations (like driving under the influence)
- have legal problems related to your drug and alcohol abuse (like arrests)
- continue to rely on drugs and alcohol, even though the chemicals are causing problems in your life

If you're addicted, you might:

- be preoccupied with obtaining alcohol and drugs
- lose control of your emotions (getting very angry or irritable)
- be unable to handle everyday responsibilities (like school, work, or extracurricular activities)
- continue to abuse despite negative consequences
- try to quit but end up abusing again
- experience symptoms of "withdrawal" when you can't get drugs or alcohol

Whether you're addicted to or abusing drugs or alcohol, you need to get help. Talk to an adult you trust (a parent, teacher, school social worker, school counselor, religious leader, or doctor). You can also look in the Yellow Pages of your phone book under "Drug Abuse," "Alcoholism," or "Mental Health" for the names of organizations and sources of help in your area. Keep trying—it may take more than one phone call to get the help you need. For more resources, see pages 67–68.

Dual Diagnosis

Drug and alcohol abuse or addiction
+ A mental health disorder
= Dual diagnosis

If you're depressed, you're more likely to abuse alcohol and other drugs. And if you abuse alcohol and other drugs, you're more likely to develop depression (it's a vicious circle). You might end up with a *dual diagnosis*—meaning you have depression and you abuse chemicals. Each condition negatively affects the other. For example, your symptoms of depression may include feeling sad, tired, and hopeless—if you use alcohol (a depressant), your painful feelings will probably intensify. People with dual disorders most often use alcohol, pot, amphetamines, heroin, or prescription painkillers.

A dual diagnosis makes you more vulnerable—you may have a harder time coping and healing. You may not respond as quickly to treatment, you could have a relapse, or you might have more medical, social, and emotional problems than other people. There *is* hope for you, though. You just have some special needs when it comes to getting help.

What treatment will work for you if you have a dual diagnosis? Some experts believe you should be treated for your depression before tackling your drug or alcohol abuse. Others say that you can't treat depression without first taking care of the chemical abuse. Then there are those who believe that the condition with the most severe symptoms should be treated first. I think that teens with a dual disorder need "integrated treatment," meaning you're treated for *both* problems at the same time by someone who has expertise in mental health and treatment of drug and alcohol abuse.

Your treatment may include:
- medication for your depression* (if necessary)
- care in a hospital or other facility to recover from your drug or alcohol abuse

*For more information about medications for depression, see pages 99–105.

- regular meetings with a healthcare provider
- talk therapy* with a trained counselor
- participation in a self-help group, with other teens who have problems like yours
- special living arrangements or changes in your diet

Getting treatment can help you get back in charge of your life. It takes time to get better, and it isn't easy. But you can make positive changes that will help you become happier and healthier.

Getting Control of Your Life

You have more control over your life than you may think. You have the power to make decisions for yourself. In fact, you make decisions every day that directly affect how you feel about yourself and your life. If you decide to get out of bed, go to school, attend class regularly, participate in activities, and do your homework, you've taken control of an important aspect of your life—school. If you talk to a trusted adult (teacher, school counselor, social worker) about your family problems, you've begun to take control of another aspect of your life—your home environment. If you choose to ask for help for a drug and alcohol problem, you're taking a step toward getting better and regaining control of the most important part of your life—*you.*

How do you get help? Talk with an adult you trust at home, at school, or in your community. The adult may recommend that you seek treatment for your depression and for drug and alcohol abuse, which means you may go to a hospital, clinic, or counselor. Getting treatment for your problems will help you take responsibility for your own life. You may have to work extra hard not to fall into the trap of abusing alcohol and drugs again.

TIP: As part of your treatment, you may take an antidepressant,** or a medication prescribed specifically for depression. If you're on an antidepressant, you should never drink alcohol or do drugs—it's dangerous and

---

*For more information about talk therapy, see pages 95–97.
**For more information about antidepressants, see pages 99–105.

can cause complications or interfere with your treatment. For example, being under the influence of drugs or alcohol might make you forget to take your medication or accidentally take too much. If this happens to you, call your caregiver right away to find out what you need to do.

Shaneeka's Story

Shaneeka, who has been diagnosed with major depression, had a rough home life. She joined a gang at age twelve, got involved with drugs and alcohol, and had trouble controlling her anger. Shaneeka was put on an antidepressant, and she started to think about changes she wanted to make in her life. While on medication, she sometimes smoked pot and drank, making it harder for her to get better. But with hard work, she was able to put that part of her life behind her.

My mom and dad were never married. I was born when my mom was fifteen and still going to high school. I bonded with my grandmother, who has been the nurturing person in my life ever since. Later, when my two sisters came along and we lived away from my grandmother, I still turned to her when I needed help, love, and support.

Growing up without a father was very hard for me. The only thing I knew about him was that he was in a gang. I was in a gang myself by the time I was twelve, and I did everything the older gang members told me to do. I skipped school, smoked marijuana, drank beer and wine, shoplifted, and robbed people. I was in and out of trouble with the law.

When I was fifteen, my mom got a new boyfriend, and she'd leave me with my younger sisters for two or three days at a time. I had the household responsibilities of cooking, cleaning, and caring for my sisters, and I still had to do my homework and keep up in school. I got very little sleep and was tired all the time. I was also very stressed out. I felt like an adult trapped in a teen's body. When I tried to talk to my mother about it, she yelled at me and wouldn't listen. My grandmother listened, though, and she stopped by with food and money when I needed it.

I was either sad or angry most of the time. Once, I got mad at one of my sisters, and I choked her. Another time, I threw her against a wall. I didn't like myself when I did those things, but I didn't know how to stop. Anger just poured out of me. My mom didn't like my behavior and asked me to see our family doctor. At first, I didn't want to go, but I eventually went. The doctor examined me, asked a lot of questions, and told me I had major depression. She put me on an antidepressant, which helped for a while, but I didn't always remember to take it. I later switched to another antidepressant, and I took it for several months, off and on. I still smoked marijuana and drank alcohol, but I didn't tell my doctor. Sometimes I felt tired and dizzy.

While I was taking the antidepressant, I started thinking about how much I disliked my life. I didn't get along with my mom, and her boyfriend made fun of my weight, which made me feel worse. As a gang member, I was doing stupid things and putting myself at risk. I was going nowhere, and I knew it was time for me to grow up—to make my life better.

The first decision I made was to get out of the gang. Then I stopped drinking alcohol and using pot. Those were hard choices, but I went through with them. Finally, I had to get out of my home environment, and I worked up the courage to leave. My grandmother let me move in with her and my grandfather, and they got temporary legal guardianship of me. I'm now going to a private school, and I no longer take medication for my depression. I still feel sad sometimes, and I have angry outbursts every now and then, but I can handle things.

I think it was good for me to get out of my depressing home environment, and I don't miss the gang life I left behind. When I feel down or have a problem, I talk to my grandmother or some of my other relatives. I'm learning to make better decisions. Someday, I hope to become a veterinarian and make a good life for myself.

"Maybe you've made mistakes. You can't change what you've done in the past, but you can make a good future for yourself. Take it one step at a time." —Shaneeka

Substance Abuse Resources

1-800-662-HELP (1-800-662-4357) connects you to the Center for Substance Abuse Treatment (CSAT) of the Substance Abuse and Mental Health Services Administration. When you dial this number, you'll hear a recording that leads to more options, such as alcohol and drug information, treatment options in your state, and counseling. Online: http://dpt.samhsa.gov

1-800-347-8998 is the number for Cocaine Anonymous. Staffers can refer you to a Cocaine Anonymous office in your area so you can join a group that meets near you. Online: www.ca.org

1-800-729-6686 is an information line for the National Clearinghouse for Alcohol and Drug Information (NCADI). This federal organization provides free information on drug and alcohol abuse. Services are available twenty-four hours a day, seven days a week. Online: http://ncadi.samhsa.gov

1-800-788-2800 will connect you to all federal alcohol and drug clearinghouses for free information on all aspects of alcohol and drugs.

Al-Anon and Alateen
www.Al-Anon.Alateen.org
This site includes information on Al-Anon, a worldwide organization designed to support families and friends of alcoholics, and Alateen (for younger members). You can find out more about the organization, decide if you want to join a group, and locate meetings in your area. By phone: 1-888-4AL-ANON (1-888-425-2666).

Freevibe
www.freevibe.com
This colorful, informative site is filled with reliable facts about drugs and has a teen chat room where you can talk about drug-related issues.

Mental Help Net
www.mentalhelp.net
This site offers information on a variety of issues, including depression and drug and alcohol abuse. Organized by subject, the site also offers ideas for finding professional help.

Web of Addictions
www.well.com/user/woa
This award-winning site features factual information on drug and alcohol abuse, including descriptions of various drugs and their effects. You'll find in-depth information, places to get help, and links to other sites.

Survival Tip #4:
Eat Good Food

"We are indeed much more than what we eat, but what we eat can nevertheless help us to be much more than what we are."
—Adelle Davis

Nutritious foods give your body and mind the fuel they need to stay healthy and strong. If you're into healthy eating, that's great. If you're a junk food fan, it's time to explore other food options. To feel balanced, you need to eat a balanced diet.

Having a balanced diet means eating plenty of foods that provide vitamins, minerals, and natural energy. You'll feel healthier if you choose:

- fresh fruits and raw veggies (steamed vegetables are a good option, too)
- dried fruits (raisins, apricots, berries)
- high-protein foods, such as eggs or lean meats like chicken or fish (choose soy products or beans and legumes if you're a vegetarian)
- whole grains (found in brown rice, whole grain bread, and whole grain pasta)
- low-fat dairy products like milk and yogurt (if you consume dairy)
- unsaturated fats in the form of plant oils (olive, canola, sunflower) or fatty fish (like salmon)

Eating a variety of healthful, wholesome foods is the best way to nourish your body. To learn more about healthy choices, check out the "Healthy Eating Pyramid," developed by the Harvard School of Public Health, which offers guidelines for eating well. (Note: Even though this pyramid suggests "alcohol in moderation," this means adults—not teens.) To view the Web page, go to: www.hsph.harvard.edu/nutrition source/pyramids.html.

The pyramid recommends not only a healthy diet but also daily exercise and weight control. You can read more about the importance of exercise on pages 15–17.

If you tend to fill up on foods that are full of fat (like cookies, candy bars, chips, and doughnuts), you'll feel weighed down and sluggish. If you're already tired because you're depressed, eating foods high in saturated fats will probably make you feel worse. Sugary products like sodas, candy, and other sweets may give you a temporary sugar buzz, but they leave you feeling wiped out and irritable because your body can't deal with all the extra sugar in your bloodstream. If you cut down on the amount of fatty and sugary foods you eat each day, you'll be healthier and more energized because you're doing something good for your body. It's fine to splurge on junk foods once in while, just try not to make high-fat foods and sweets a staple of your diet.

And speaking of sweets, watch for artificial sweeteners (like aspartame and sucralose, which appear under the product names Nutra-Sweet and Splenda). If you drink diet sodas, you're probably consuming artificial sweeteners on a regular basis. Some people seem to have physical reactions to these sweeteners, including headaches or feeling shaky. Eliminating artificial sweeteners could help you feel better.

Sometimes it's hard to resist eating foods that aren't very healthy. Eating can be an emotional activity, and food that tastes good often makes you feel better while you're eating it. Think about the "comfort foods" you turn to when you're feeling anxious, sad, or upset. Maybe when you're feeling down, you crave chocolate; when you're worried or stressed out, you might reach for high-fat junk foods or a sugary drink. When you "need" comfort foods, ask yourself if something is bothering you. Instead of grabbing a bag of potato chips, pick up the phone and call a friend to share what's on your mind or talk to your parents, if you feel comfortable doing so. You may want to ask the person who does the food shopping at your home not to buy as many high-fat or sugary foods and to stock up on fresh fruits, vegetables, and low-fat snacks—this way, you won't be tempted to eat junk food as often.

Changing your diet is a good way to improve your mood and outlook, but you have to be careful not to go overboard. Avoid going on a diet where you constantly deprive yourself of foods you really want. The added pressure will probably make you feel more anxious and stressed out. Eating healthy is much different than dieting. When you eat healthy, you make a conscious effort to consume more fresh, wholesome foods and cut down on products that offer little nutritional value, like caffeinated drinks and junk foods. Dieting, on the other hand, usually means cutting your calorie intake, always watching your weight, and feeling guilty when you put food in your mouth (all of which can stress you out and contribute to depression).

When you diet excessively, you run the risk of getting an eating disorder like anorexia nervosa or bulimia nervosa (another one is compulsive overeating disorder). Eating disorders, which have been linked to depression, are serious, life-threatening illnesses. If you're starving yourself, binging on food and then throwing it up, or stuck in a cycle of overeating and dieting, you need to get help. Talk to someone you trust—a parent, a school counselor, or your doctor—and let the person know that you have a problem with eating. If you can't talk to someone face-to-face, you can contact one of the national resources on page 71 or call a Crisis Hotline listed in your Yellow Pages.

Eating Disorder Resources

(847) 831-3438 connects you to the National Association of Anorexia Nervosa and Associated Disorders (ANAD). They are available Monday through Friday 9 A.M. to 5 P.M. CST. This organization provides help to people with eating disorders and their families. ANAD's free services include access to a network of support groups and referral sources, a newsletter, and educational programs. Online: www.anad.org

1-800-931-2237 is the number for the National Eating Disorders Association, an educational, treatment, and referral resource for people with eating disorders, their families, and healthcare professionals. Online: www.nationaleatingdisorders.org

(505) 891-2664 contacts the World Service Office of Overeaters Anonymous. You can call their offices Monday through Friday 8 A.M. to 4:30 P.M. MST for information on this twelve-step group. The program helps overeaters, as well as those with anorexia or bulimia. Online: www.oa.org

Ways to be good to yourself:

- Start your day with a good breakfast. Eating something in the morning—even just yogurt, fruit, or a piece of toast—will boost your energy level and help you face the day.
- Take a multivitamin every day to supplement your diet, but don't use vitamins as a substitute for fruits and vegetables.
- Avoid caffeine (in coffee, lattes, sodas, etc.) because it can make you feel nervous or anxious. Although caffeine may give you quick energy, the effects soon wear off and can leave you feeling more tired later.
- Since you alone are in charge of what goes into your body, you can choose not to use alcohol, pot, and other drugs. They'll sabotage everything you do to stay well.
- Drink herbal teas to relax. Try chamomile or other flavors; mix in some lemon or honey for added natural flavor.
- Drink lots of water each day (8–12 cups). Water quenches your thirst, hydrates your body, and flushes out your system.

- Taking a daily fish-oil supplement has been shown to be helpful for some depressed people. Fish oil contains omega-3 fatty acids (known for their heart-healthy effects) and may help alleviate anxiety and sleep problems. Talk to your doctor to get more information first.

- Sunflower seeds and pumpkin seeds contain a natural anti-depressant called tryptophan. Snacking on them can help you feel calm.

CHAPTER

"I knew if I didn't get help, I would die.
I went to a trusted teacher." —Gretchen, 17

Depression
and
Suicide

Brian was one of the neighborhood kids who hung out at my house when my sons were growing up. His handsome face and sunny smile masked the sadness he felt about his parents' divorce. When Brian was in seventh grade, he left our neighborhood to live with his father, and I saw him only occasionally after that.

During his teen years, Brian was depressed, and he isolated himself, flew into rages, and abused drugs and alcohol to cope with his painful feelings. His family tried to help, but they couldn't get through to him. One fall day, when Brian was eighteen, he drove his car into the loading dock of a building a few miles away and died. His death was a complete shock to everyone who knew him, including me.

At the time, no one had understood the clues that Brian left about his suicide. No one realized how much he needed—and wanted—help. Some of Brian's behaviors prior to his suicide were typical of someone planning to die—he listened to sad music, drew morbid pictures, and made cryptic statements like "You won't have to worry about me any-more. . . ." In retrospect, the people who loved Brian realized that the clues were messages about what he planned to do.

73

Why Would Anyone Want to Die?

There aren't any easy answers to this question. Experts estimate that, each year, about 500,000 young people try to kill themselves; about 4,000 of them actually die. So, on average, eleven teens complete suicide each day. According to the National Institute of Mental Health, suicide is the third leading cause of death (after homicide and motor vehicle accidents) in young people ages fifteen to twenty-four. Suicide is a frightening, confusing issue—one that most people don't want to talk about.

It's important to understand that:
1. Most suicidal teens DON'T REALLY WANT TO DIE.
2. Talking about suicide is *a way to help a suicidal person.*

Teens who want to kill themselves are trying to escape problems that seem too overwhelming to solve. The tragedy is that they choose a *permanent* solution to *temporary* problems. This is why it's so important to talk about suicide, not sweep it under the rug. When teens get their feelings out in the open and ask for help, suddenly the problems don't seem so big and so awful. Having a concerned and caring person say "I will help you" can play a big role in reversing suicidal thoughts.

Suicide is a response to feeling hopeless, helpless, alone, and worthless—all these feelings are linked to depression. In fact, people with depression are thirty times more likely to complete suicide than other people. Even someone who is mildly depressed may be thinking about suicide.

If you have considered suicide or are thinking about it now, GET HELP. Please do it immediately! Tell an adult you trust—a parent, relative, teacher, school counselor, religious leader, doctor, or mental health professional.

You can also call 911 or go to a hospital emergency room (take a taxi or ask a friend to drive you). If you're by yourself and you don't want to talk to someone face-to-face, find your Yellow Pages and look for a Suicide Hotline or Crisis Hotline. On page 82, you'll find a list of national resources you can contact. Take care of yourself right now.

Trust that the person you talk to won't judge you.

Believe that you don't need to act on suicidal thoughts at this time. Suicidal thoughts will pass, but you need to get help.

Please call for help now.

Crisis Resource

1-800-448-3000 is the number for the Girls and Boys Town National Hotline, a national Crisis Hotline you can call anytime, twenty-four hours a day. You'll talk to a professional counselor who will listen and give you advice on any issue (depression, suicide, identity struggles, family troubles, and other problems). Online: www.girlsandboystown.org/hotline

How do you start a conversation when you're feeling hopeless or thinking about wanting to die?

You Can Say:

- "I'm not feeling safe right now. Can we talk about how I feel?"
- "I need to talk about how I've been feeling lately. I'm having thoughts about dying, and I want them to stop."
- "Will you look at this poem I wrote? It tells how I'm feeling."
- "I feel bad, and I can't think of a reason to go on living."
- "I'm afraid of the thoughts I'm having. I need someone to help me."

Ryland's Story

Eighteen-year-old Ryland seemed like he had everything going for him. He had lots of friends, had a part-time job, played saxophone in the jazz band, ran cross-country, wrestled, surfed, and belonged to the Civil Air Patrol. He volunteered once a week at a senior center, where he hung out with a group of elderly women (he called them his "Grannies"), reading stories and teaching them to play pool. But Ryland was depressed; inside he felt angry, sad, and desperate, and he didn't know how to talk about these feelings. His mother tells Ryland's story because he's unable to tell it himself.

My son, Ryland, and his father were very close. They shared a love of outdoor sports and spent a lot of time together. One morning when Ryland was eleven, his father went for a bike ride and never returned. He had died of a heart attack. Ryland went to grief counseling, and I coped with depression. Somehow we got on with our lives.

I remarried three years later, and Ryland and his stepfather got along well. We soon moved to the city, away from Ryland's lifelong friends. Around the time of the move, Ryland's behavior changed. He began to isolate himself; he withdrew. When I confronted him, he insisted nothing was wrong. If I questioned him further, he'd get angry, yell, cry, and refuse to talk to me. He agreed to see a counselor but only went twice.

By his sophomore year, Ryland was going through some scary changes. He wouldn't eat dinner with us anymore, and he stayed in his room a lot with the door closed. By senior year, he was thinking about college and wanted to go to Long Beach State, in California. When he wasn't accepted there, he felt personally rejected and refused to consider any other school. Eventually, he decided to study filmmaking at a local community college the following fall. He still spent a lot of time alone in his bedroom, listening to sad songs.

Ryland's stepfather told me he thought Ryland was depressed. I was shocked. I hadn't identified Ryland's behaviors as signs of depression, but I remembered times when I would stop by Ryland's room to talk, and he would slip something under his futon. I wondered if this could give me a clue about what was going on. One morning, I secretly reached under the futon and drew out a notebook filled with dark, sad, morbid poetry about life not being worth living. I realized Ryland was suicidal, and I couldn't understand why. He was smart and good looking—he had everything going for him. I replaced the notebook and didn't tell Ryland I'd looked at it. His graduation was coming up, and his relatives were arriving from California to celebrate. We were going to have a special family party for him.

I wrote Ryland a loving and positive letter the next day, telling him that I knew life was scary sometimes but that college would be a great adventure. I also told him I knew he was thinking about suicide and that I didn't know what I'd do if I lost him. When Ryland came home, I asked him to sit with me. I had his notebook in my hands. I asked him, "Are you thinking about killing yourself?" He looked right into my eyes and said he had been thinking about it but wasn't anymore. I asked him to read my letter. He read it, stood up, walked into his room, and closed the door.

This was a busy and emotional time for Ryland. The anniversary of his father's death occurred four weeks before his graduation; his eighteenth birthday followed two weeks after the anniversary. At his graduation party, which took place the night before the ceremony, Ryland was there, but at the same time he wasn't. He sort of just floated around talking to people, but he didn't seem to be enjoying himself. The next day, we were surprised to see that Ryland carried the class colors in the graduation ceremony—he hadn't mentioned he'd been chosen for this honor.

Everything exploded a few days later when Ryland's stepfather and I tried to discuss what Ryland would do for spending money in college. Ryland became really upset and began to yell. It was as though all the hurt and anger inside him came to the surface in that instant. He ran to his room and started blasting music. We followed him and found him ripping posters, awards, and pictures off his walls. He threw his stereo into his mirror, shattering it. When he raised his fists to fight his stepdad, I told him to get out of the house. He took his backpack and left.

Later that night, there was a knock on the door. I opened it, and two police-men stood on the steps. I knew instantly that something terrible had happened. They said Ryland had jumped off a nearby bridge and was still alive in one of Seattle's top trauma centers. For the next four months, Ryland was in a coma.

Today, Ryland communicates by poking a computer keyboard with one finger; a synthesized "voice" then speaks from a box. He's in a wheelchair and can't walk, and he eats pureed food. He needs help to go to the bathroom, bathe, and dress.

With time and work, Ryland has developed his thinking skills enough to be aware of his situation. Sometimes he still feels depressed, but other times he talks about going to college, getting married, and having children. We take it a day at a time.

> **"I hope that if you're suicidal, you'll get help as soon as possible. If you feel alone, misunderstood, or depressed, talk to someone about it. Help is available— just ask for it."** —Ryland's mom

Nobody Really Wants to Die

When a depressed teen says "I want to die," all of us need to hear "I'm feeling so alone (helpless, hopeless, worthless) right now, it's unbear-able. I can't think of any way to escape these painful feelings except to die." Usually, suicidal people are so focused on emotional pain that they aren't able to think of anything good about themselves or their lives. They want to live, but they need help coping and considering ways to solve their problems. Fortunately, suicidal thinking is usually temporary. There's a chance to get help—a way to survive and have a better life.

"It's scary to think where I might be now without the help I got. Even though I'm nineteen now and consider myself an adult, I found I was unable to manage depression without help. It took me nearly a year of crying myself to sleep at night after my fiancé broke our engagement. I wasn't even mentally 'there' at my graduation from high school. I lost a lot of weight and had occasional thoughts of suicide. I forced myself to make an appointment with a psychologist, and it has been a life-changing experience for me. I hope other teens will find someone to help them sooner than I did." —April, 19

A person who threatens suicide feels desperate and is asking for help. Rarely does anyone plan suicide without giving clues of some kind. Sometimes the clues are very subtle. In fact, family members and friends may completely miss or misinterpret them.

Suicide Danger Signals

Following are danger signals that indicate someone may be considering suicide. *Clues or hints of suicide should always be taken very seriously.*

Suicide clues might include:
- previous suicide attempts
- statements about feeling hopeless, helpless, or worthless
- statements about being a burden to others
- threats of suicide (direct or indirect)
- a loss of interest in activities
- behavior or statements that indicate "good-byes"
- talking about death
- listening to songs about death, or drawing or writing about death
- using alcohol/drugs, driving too fast, or doing other risky things
- giving away valued possessions

Sometimes people don't know how to respond to the warning signs of suicide—they don't take action because they simply don't know that they should. Why don't people know what to do? When we see someone clutch his chest, fall to the floor, and stop breathing, we know to perform CPR (cardiopulmonary resuscitation) or call for help right away. If someone's choking to death, we know that the Heimlich maneuver is a life-saving technique. But few people know about the warning signs of suicide—and the life-saving actions that could help in an emergency. Part of the problem is that suicide is a scary topic that people tend to ignore or hide from. One way to prevent suicide is to discuss it.

If someone is hinting about suicide, *talk about it.* Saying the word "suicide" won't give someone the idea to go through with it. Talking about suicide can help a suicidal person think of other options. Assume that the person is serious, even if you've heard the suicide threats before and nothing happened—you can never be sure about someone's intentions *this* time.

What to do if someone threatens suicide:

- Stay calm.
- Tell the person that you're taking his or her feelings seriously and want to help.
- Show concern and ask caring questions. Listen to the answers.
- Reassure the person that you know how to get help.
- Stay close to the person while you tell a trusted, responsible adult that help is needed.
- If it's safe for you, remove items that the person could use for suicide. Remain with the person until professional help is available.

Following are some things you can say to calm or reassure a suicidal person.

You Can Say:

- "Is there some way I can help you to feel safer right now?"
- "I'm going to stay here with you for a while. I'm a good listener."
- "Can you tell me what it's like for you—feeling this way?"
- "I'm feeling afraid for you, and I'm going to help you find help."
- "Tell me what's been happening for the past few days."

You can also help the person call a Suicide Hotline listed in the Yellow Pages (for more numbers, see the resources on pages 75 and 82).

When calling you can say:

- "Hello, I'm with my friend (cousin, brother/sister, neighbor) who's feeling very depressed right now, and we need help immediately."
- "I'm with someone who's thinking about suicide. Please tell us what we should do."
- "I'm with someone who's feeling hopeless about his/her life. We need to talk to someone right away."

Following is what NOT to do when someone is suicidal:

- Don't assume the person is "just trying to get attention." Give the person the benefit of the doubt.
- Don't challenge the person to "go ahead and do it," because this increases the danger of it actually happening.
- Don't promise the person that you won't tell anyone. A suicidal person needs to know you care enough to get help right away.
- Don't try to tell the person how to feel. Just show you care by saying that you want to help.
- Don't try to argue someone out of feeling suicidal (a person can't help feeling this way).
- Don't say that suicide is "dumb" or that the person should "snap out of it." Making judgments is harmful, not helpful.

Suicide Resources

American Association of Suicidology
5221 Wisconsin Avenue, NW
Washington, DC 20015
(202) 237-2280
www.suicidology.org
This association offers pamphlets about suicide and referrals to support groups around the country.

Covenant House Nineline
1-800-999-9999
www.nineline.org
The Nineline provides immediate crisis intervention, support, and referrals for runaways, abandoned youth, and those who are suicidal or in crisis. Help is available for children, teens, and adults.

National Hopeline Network
1-800-784-2433
This national hotline is available twenty-four hours a day, seven days a week. Counselors are available to talk or offer referrals to local mental health professionals.

Suicide Awareness Voices of Education (SAVE)
www.save.org
At this Web site you'll find warning signs of suicide, support for suicide survivors, and more. It includes "Friends and Depression: A Guide for Young People."

Teens at Risk

Calvin, a handsome African American boy of fifteen, lived with his parents and two sisters in an affluent suburban neighborhood. He went to a mostly white high school, where he served as president of his freshman class and excelled in academics and sports. He was making plans to realize his dream of becoming a professional football player. Calvin had the usual sibling disagreements but got along well with his family. He loved to wrestle playfully with their dog, Woof.

One afternoon, Calvin arrived home from school at the usual time after football practice. His mom was fixing dinner. His father, a physician, wasn't home from work yet. Calvin greeted his mother, then went upstairs to his bedroom and shot himself to death. No one expected this to happen. No one thought Calvin was at risk for suicide. Calvin's family and friends didn't think he had any problems he couldn't solve.

Calvin's suicide reflects a trend in teen suicides in the United States. While youth suicides occur most frequently among white males between the ages of fifteen and twenty-four, the rate among African-American males is on the rise. The increase in suicides among young black males could be a result of increased drug use, family problems, and the stress of achieving middle-class success—problems that often lead to feelings of depression and hopelessness.

"I am still trying to understand why my brother killed himself. We were very close, and it hurt me so bad. I am reading about suicide and seeing a counselor about my depression. It will take a long time to feel 'normal' again. Someday, I hope I can be a counselor to help other kids when they're hurting." —Wendy, 12

Research also shows that the rate of suicide attempts among Hispanic girls is on the rise, with an estimated one in five trying to take their own lives.[5] Many of these young women don't actually want to die but may impulsively swallow pills or cut themselves because they can't find ways to cope with the conflicts and troubles they face every day. Many feel caught in a cultural clash—they're required to live by their family's strict traditional values at home, but in the larger world, they have more freedoms and a whole different set of expectations. Studies show that one in four Hispanic girls report having symptoms of depression; however, because of language or economic barriers, many never get the help they need.

Among ethnic groups, Native American teens have the highest rates of depression and suicide. Issues of tribal identity and feelings of "Where do I belong?" affect almost all Native American youth. According to Riki Jacobs, a Native American mental health specialist and a member of the Choctaw Nation, Native teens can suffer from a type of depression known as *anomic* depression. This means your depression is caused, in part, by struggling with who you are and where you belong culturally. If you're a Native American teen and you feel depressed, are using alcohol and/or other drugs, or are feeling stuck somewhere between your culture and a larger, dominant culture, talk to an adult you trust. Look to a parent, a tribal elder, a teacher, or any other adult who can offer guidance and support.

Heather's Story

Fifteen-year-old Heather has been diagnosed with bipolar disorder. She's the second of three girls in her family, and the only one with red hair and very fair skin. Her father is Native American, and her mother is Caucasian. Although Heather's family practices Native American cultural traditions, she has never felt accepted by either the dominant white culture or the Indian culture, and this identity struggle has contributed to her depression.

My first real friend, Angela, died when we were in fifth grade, and I didn't know what to do about my grief. I wished I could trade places with her. That's when I first started thinking about suicide. Around that time, my family moved to a small, mostly white community. I wanted my classmates to accept me as Native American, but they saw my fair skin and red hair and didn't believe I was Indian. I said I hated white people because I thought it would make the white kids believe I was Indian and the Native kids accept me (they didn't). I felt like I didn't belong in either culture—I was totally alone.

By sixth grade, I not only thought about suicide but also started to plan ways to do it. I had no friends—none. I rarely talked to Native people. After school, I was just the shy little redheaded Indian at the Tribal Center, whose dad was active in tribal business matters. When I joined a dance group and learned to perform traditional tribal dances, I thought I'd finally found a place to belong. After we began performing publicly, though, someone would always ask, "What are you doing in a Native dance group? You're not Indian." I felt like a phony and thought my life would always be this way; I felt hopeless about everything.

During the summer after seventh grade, I won the title of Miss Chief Seattle Days for my tribe. I thought it would be the greatest year of my life, but it turned out to be the absolute worst. While I was representing my tribe at the Salmon Homecoming Pow-wow, a photographer for a major Seattle newspaper wanted to take a picture of some of the princesses, but he said to me, "Not you, you're not Indian." That hurt so much. My grades were slipping, and this saddened me even more because I've always been serious about going to college. Someday I'd like to become a journalist and start a magazine.

One of my duties as Miss Chief Seattle Days was to go to New Mexico to represent my tribe at the United Indian Nations Pow-wow— the biggest Pow-wow in the world. The whole experience was torture for me. Kids laughed at me and called me names. Adults smirked and argued with me about my heritage. I got sick, and it didn't help to be stuffed into an arena with thousands of people each day. I wore a beautiful dress made of cedar, but I was so ill that I cried while people were taking my picture. I was so nervous that I broke out in hives. During the entire five-day ordeal, I only saw one other biracial princess, and she was rude to me, too. I was glad to return home.

During my reign as Miss Chief Seattle Days, I volunteered to be involved in a project to promote awareness of teen pregnancy. As part of a Public Service Announcement, I helped write a video production, and I acted in it, too. It won first place in the state of Washington. We also won an Emmy at the Television Emmy Awards in Seattle, and I should have been thrilled, but it didn't mean anything to me because I was so miserable inside.

Following a suicide attempt that year, I began seeing a therapist with expertise in adolescent mental health. I found it easier to talk to my therapist about my feelings than to anyone else. She told me I have bipolar disorder, and she put me on an antidepressant and a mood stabilizer. My diagnosis was a relief because I finally understood some of the reasons behind my feelings and behavior.

> **"You don't really want to die—you want a way out of feeling alone. You can learn ways to cope with your hurts."** —Heather

Several months ago, I decided a second time to die, but I changed my mind just in time. My therapist helped me tell my parents about what I was going through and showed me how to deal with my feelings of not belonging anywhere. Finally, I'm learning to be proud of both parts of me, white and Indian.

Survival Tip #5:
Talk About It

"Not everything that is faced can be changed. But nothing can be changed until it is faced." —James Baldwin

One of the terrible things about depression is that it causes such painful feelings, like sadness, anger, and hopelessness. You may withdraw from people who care about you because you think they won't understand what you're going through. Or you might isolate yourself so that it's just you and your painful feelings. When you get to this point, you may feel even more desperate and discouraged.

Feelings need to be felt—even if you don't like them. If you keep your emotions bottled up inside, they can hurt you and make you feel even worse. Facing your feelings and talking about them, on the other hand, is a good release.

Ways to face your feelings:

- When you can't seem to think straight, stop thinking and *feel*. Becoming aware of your feelings helps you sort through them.
- When you're afraid, *breathe*. Take a few slow, deep breaths until you calm down a little, then talk to someone you trust.
- If you're angry, say it with words or write it down, instead of acting out.
- When you're sad, cry.
- When you're lonely, call or visit someone.
- Know this about your feelings: If you can feel them, you can heal them.

One of the best ways to deal with painful emotions and start healing is to talk to someone you trust. Talking to someone who will listen and understand is a way to put things into perspective. You'll see that you aren't as alone as you may think. It might feel scary to talk to someone about what's bothering you, but you can do it. Find an adult you trust (a parent, teacher, or family friend). If you need suggestions for how to tell someone you're hurting, see page 75.

You may find it helpful to keep a list of people to contact when you're feeling desperate and alone. This way, no matter where you are, you can phone someone to let the person know how you're feeling. You can copy the form on page 88 and write down the names and numbers of people you can call (ask them beforehand if you can put them on your list, so they aren't taken by surprise). Keep these numbers with you in your cell phone, wallet, purse, or backpack, in case you start to feel upset or need to talk to someone.

Important Numbers

The adult I trust the most
to listen to me and help me is: _____

Work phone: _____ Home phone: _____

Cell phone: _____

Address: _____

Another helpful adult is: _____

Work phone: _____ Home phone: _____

Cell phone: _____

Address: _____

Other people who can help:

Name: _____ Number(s): _____

Name: _____ Number(s): _____

Name: _____ Number(s): _____

The number of my local crisis center is: _____

part 2: Getting Help and Staying Well

"When you have a great and difficult task, if you only work a little at a time, every day a little, suddenly the work will finish itself." —Isak Dinesen

"I was crying a lot at home. The coach started asking me questions, and I got help." —Kevin, 17

Who and What Can Help

When you have depression, you may feel so bad that it doesn't seem possible to ever feel better (it *is* possible, though). Depression may leave you exhausted, helpless, discouraged, and hopeless—making it much harder for you to seek help. In fact, you may need *help* getting help.

It's important to find a trained professional who understands *teen* depression. Some teens hide their feelings so it's hard to know whether they're depressed; other teens numb themselves with drugs and alcohol, which can mask depressive symptoms. Parents, teachers, and other adults may not realize that the problem is depression. Many teens act out their distress (through anger, aggression, running away, or delinquency), and it may take a mental health professional to see this behavior as a cry for help. An expert can help you find out if your feelings, moods, and behaviors are related to depression.

Getting help works. In fact, with appropriate treatment, more than 80 percent of people with depression can feel good again and return to their normal daily activities—usually within a few weeks. But it's important to get an accurate diagnosis as soon as possible after your symptoms start—and find a treatment that works for *you*. No

two people experience depression in exactly the same way.
For some, the symptoms are
severe and long-lasting; for
others, they're milder. You
can't know for sure what
you're dealing with until you
get a professional diagnosis.
Think of it this way: If you
had a broken leg, would you
try to set it yourself? Of course
not! You'd see an expert to get
the care you need.

**If you want to get professional help, you can see one of the
following types of experts who offer treatment and care for
depression:**

- **Psychiatrists** are medical doctors who specialize in mental
  health. They assess people, administer tests, diagnose mental
  illness, prescribe medications, and provide therapy.

- **Clinical Psychologists** are experts in human behavior who
  assess people, administer tests, diagnose mental illness, and
  provide therapy.

- **Psychiatric Nurse Practitioners** are registered nurses trained
  to deal with mental disorders. They assess people, administer
  tests, diagnose mental illness, prescribe medications, and provide therapy.

- **Clinical Social Workers** have advanced training in social work,
  with an emphasis on mental health. They can provide you and
  your family with help and information.

- **General Physicians** may be the first to identify a mental health
  problem after a physical examination, and may refer you to a
  specialist for further help.

- **Psychotherapists** and **Counselors** are trained to listen to you
  and help you make changes in yourself and your life.

Many other kinds of help are available, too:

- **Crisis Centers** offer immediate help to individuals or families who need it. If you're suicidal or if your family is abusive, for example, a crisis center can provide counseling and care. Crisis counselors are usually mental health professionals trained to listen and find further help for you.

- **Crisis Hotlines** are staffed by mental health professionals or trained volunteers who listen to your problems and recommend other sources of help. Most hotlines are open twenty-four hours a day; look in your Yellow Pages for numbers.

- **Religious Leaders** can give you spiritual counsel and comfort.

- **Self-Help Groups** are support groups of people who share a similar problem. Some groups are run by a mental health professional, while others aren't. The group members discuss their feelings, encourage each other, and suggest ways to cope.

- **Twelve-Step Groups** (such as Alcoholics Anonymous) are self-help groups that follow a specific program, meet in a variety of locations day and night, don't charge participants a fee, and can be found in nearly every city. These groups have a spiritual emphasis and believe that a higher power can help guide you to recovery.

- **Residential Care** can mean a group home, halfway house, hospital, or shelter for runaways. This kind of care is helpful if your family is in a crisis because you're able to work through your problems away from home in a calmer environment.

- **Adolescent Treatment Units (ATUs)** help young people heal and cope with their feelings. ATUs are sometimes part of community mental health service agencies or are located in hospitals; some ATUs are privately owned and operated. An ATU staff usually includes psychiatrists, psychologists, nurses, and counselors.

"I spent quite a bit of time in a residential treatment facility because I was having such a hard time wanting to stay alive. I've been sad and angry ever since I can remember. It's been hard for me, but I'm learning to face my issues and I want to face the world again. Where I want to be a year from now is at home, going to school, and making friends who understand me. I can't say I enjoyed being in an institution, but at least I know that it has given me another way to think about my life." —Jamie, 15

Treating Depression

Finding the right treatment for you depends on:

1. how severe your symptoms are
2. how long you've had your symptoms
3. your treatment preferences
4. the advice of your doctor or mental health professional

You'll first need to see a physician who can give you a medical exam because your symptoms could be related to another physical illness and not depression. After other medical disorders have been ruled out, you can visit a mental health professional, who might ask you to complete one or more simple questionnaires. Your answers will help the mental health professional determine whether you have depression, what kind you may have, and the types of treatment that will work best for you. It's important to be honest and as accurate as you can be when you're filling out the forms.

You may be asked about:

- your family history
- whether you, a parent, and another close relative have ever had depression
- your home life
- your relationships with friends and family members

- your school environment, grades, and peer relationships
- any traumatic experiences in your life
- your appetite and eating habits
- your use of drugs and/or alcohol

You don't have to feel embarrassed about answering these personal questions; mental health professionals want to help you, not judge you. Just say what's true for you.

Can I Afford Treatment?

Talk to a parent about the kind of medical insurance your family has, so you can find out whether you're insured for mental health treatment. If you don't have insurance, or if your insurance doesn't cover the costs of treatment or only pays a portion of it, you might consider seeking help at a community health or mental health service agency in your area. These agencies often provide counseling (and medication, if you need it) on a sliding-scale arrangement, which means you pay only what you can afford. To find out more about mental health resources in your area, contact a local Crisis Hotline and explain your situation to a staff member. National mental health organizations (see page 134) can help families find sources of financial aid for mental health issues.

Psychotherapy (Talk Therapy)

Whether you see a psychiatrist, a psychologist, or another mental health professional, you'll probably get "psychotherapy." No, this doesn't mean you're a psycho! Psychotherapy, also known as "talk therapy," is individual, family, or group therapy (or a combination of these). It's a way to talk about your problems.

Talk therapy can often resolve milder types of depression. During the sessions, you might focus on personal relationships (this is known as "Interpersonal Therapy," or IPT), especially if your depression may have been triggered, in part, by a separation from a parent, problems with authority, or intense peer pressure. In IPT, you learn to identify your individual difficulties in relating to others and develop skills to resolve them. You work on figuring out ways to better communicate and interact with family members, friends, peers, and the authority figures in your life.

Or, you might focus on Cognitive Behavioral Therapy (CBT), which helps you change negative thinking and behaviors. The main idea is that *what you think* affects *how you feel*. Put another way, the words you tell yourself (your "self-talk") can help you or hurt you. Here's an example: Suppose you have to give an oral report, and you're nervous (like anyone would be). But you tell yourself "I'm no good" or "No matter how much I practice, I'll look like an idiot." With messages like that spinning around in your head, your anxiety increases—you feel defeated before you even start. On the other hand, telling yourself "Yeah, I'm nervous but that's normal" or "This is a hard assignment so it's going to take some extra energy to do it well" makes it easier to succeed. CBT can be effective if you're depressed because the goal is not only to change negativity and hurtful self-talk, but also to learn to see life (and yourself) in a more positive light.

Talk therapy usually lasts about 10 to 20 weeks, with sessions once a week or more. The therapy *can* help, but you have to make the most of it. Some teens feel embarrassed about going to therapy because they think it's a waste of time, a sign of weakness, or a form of punishment. They may believe they're better off working out their problems on their own. Therapy isn't something to be ashamed of—it's worked for millions of people, and it can work for you, too.

Most therapists will spend 15 minutes or more with you at no cost, so you can see if you feel comfortable talking with them. If you don't interact well with the person for whatever reason, you can find someone else. After you choose a therapist you like, go to at least three sessions to decide if the person is someone you want to continue seeing.

Ask yourself these questions:

- Am I comfortable with this therapist?
- Does he or she really listen and understand?
- Do I trust this person?
- Do I believe that she or he can help me?

If you don't think the therapist is right for you after three sessions, talk to a parent about your concerns; your dad or mom may be able to help you figure out if you should find a new therapist or give the current one another chance. When you're thinking about changing therapists, ask yourself if it's the *therapist* you feel uncomfortable with or the *process of therapy.* Opening up to a stranger and talking about your painful feelings may be difficult for you. Having doubts is natural. Learn to trust the process—it works.

Another option is family therapy—which can take place in addition to your individual IPT or CBT. Family therapy is especially helpful if you're depressed because of family conflict. You could also explore group therapy, which takes place among a group of unrelated people who share their problems and feelings with the help of a trained mental health professional.

Look at therapy as a chance to express your feelings without anyone judging you—a way to make positive changes in your life. Therapy is an opportunity to learn to control how you think, act, and feel—to be a happier person. You won't be "cured" in two or three weeks, but you'll start to feel better. Give it time.

Teen Resource

It's Kind of a Funny Story: A Novel by Ned Vizzini (Miramax, 2006). Ned Vizzini is a successful young author who happens to know a lot about depression—because as a teen he was depressed and spent time in a psychiatric hospital. His experiences helped him craft this funny, poignant novel about Craig Gilner, a depressed teen who calls a suicide hotline and checks into a psychiatric hospital, where he gets therapy, examines his feelings, and finds the will to survive. The hopeful, powerful ending is a personal message to any teen struggling with depression or suicidal feelings.

MacKenzie's Story

Sixteen-year-old MacKenzie has major depression, which led to feelings of discouragement and isolation. She started seeing a therapist for help with sorting out her feelings and putting her problems into perspective. MacKenzie hopes to someday become a school counselor to help young people with problems like the ones she's faced herself.

The trouble started when I turned sixteen. Everything hit me at once: working hard to get good grades, wanting my parents to be proud of me, feeling the pressure of competition in sports, and worrying about boys. I just didn't know how to handle the stress, and I turned to marijuana. I'd skip school to get high, and I didn't think about the consequences.

I was on the volleyball team, and we signed a contract not to use drugs or alcohol during the playing season. The coach noticed that I was having bad days. He'd tell me I looked really down, and he'd ask if I wanted to talk about it. I'd just tell him nothing was wrong. He opened every door he could for me, and I pulled them all shut. I wouldn't talk to anyone about how awful I was feeling or how I wasn't eating or sleeping very well. For a couple of months, it was easier to go home and go to bed than deal with things.

I didn't feel safe telling anyone how I felt. I didn't want my parents to be ashamed of me, and I didn't want to be a burden on my friends. I wouldn't talk to my school counselor, either. I simply separated myself from all the people who cared about me because it felt safer to be alone.

One day, the coach approached me and said that someone on the team had told him I'd been high at one of our games. The dam broke wide open. I was desperate for someone to know what was going on inside me, so I told him everything, and it felt great to talk to someone who cared. I was suspended from the team, and I had to tell my parents the truth about what happened, but this helped me to get help.

I started to see a thera-pist who was very easy to talk to. She didn't judge what I said, did, or felt. She was objective and listened

"Please don't think you're the only one feeling this way. Don't be alone and hurting. I hope you'll take a chance and trust someone enough to let them help you." —MacKenzie

without getting emotional, and I could take suggestions from her more easily than I could from my parents. Whenever I was com-pletely confused about my feelings, she helped me identify them and clarify my thoughts. She also helped me work through my problems. It really helped to have a therapist who would listen and understand.

Medications for Depression

"I have been taking an antidepressant and seeing a psychia-trist each month. I am making an effort to read as much as I can about depression. I try to focus on what I love—art and music—whenever I feel destructive toward myself. Being depressed is a struggle, but I'm dealing with it the best way I can." —Elizabeth, 16

For some depressed people, a combination approach works best—therapy plus a prescription medication that may help reduce the symp-toms of depression. The medications used to treat major depression are called *antidepressants*. You already may be aware that antidepres-sants are prescribed much more often today than they were in the past. You may also know that the use of antidepressants among teens is a controversial issue.

Here are three things you should know about antidepressant medications:

1. They're used for more severe depression.

2. They're useful when other strategies have proven unsuccessful.

3. They're only part of the treatment—other therapies are still important.

Your mental health professional will need to diagnose the kind of depression you have before deciding whether medication is the best choice for you. Because you're still a teen, your parents will play a role in helping to decide whether medication might be an effective treatment and what type of antidepressant you can take. It's crucial that you don't try to obtain these types of prescription medications on your own (for example, using someone else's medication or trying to order prescription drugs over the Internet). Antidepressant use among teens and children is now carefully monitored by the Food and Drug Administration (FDA), and for good reason.

In the past few years, several highly publicized studies showed that a small percentage of children and teens may experience an increase in suicidal thoughts while taking an antidepressant medication. The studies led the FDA to recommend that warning labels be placed on the packaging of all antidepressants (whether prescribed for children, teens, or adults). Researchers have continued to study whether suicidal thoughts truly *do* increase for young people taking antidepressants—and why. At this time, it isn't clear whether the suicidal thoughts are linked to the medications' side effects or something else. It's still important to note that many young people *do* seem to respond positively to medications for depression.

Before getting a prescription for an antidepressant medication, it's helpful to know what to expect. Don't be afraid to speak up and ask questions.

Make sure you know:

- the reasons for taking the medication
- what relief you can expect

- other possible treatments
- potential side effects (reactions)
- what to do if you have suicidal thoughts (Chapter 5 covers this topic)
- who is responsible for monitoring you and for how long

How do antidepressants work? They increase the availability of certain brain chemicals* (such as serotonin), which helps regulate your thinking, emotions, and behavior. Altogether, there are four classes of antidepressants—tricyclic antidepressants (TCAs), monoamine oxidase inhibitors (MAOIs), selective serotonin reuptake inhibitors (SSRIs), and serotonin/norepinephrine reuptake inhibitors (SNRIs). SSRIs and SNRIs are most often prescribed for teens because these medications are generally considered safer, and they have fewer side effects than other antidepressants.

About half of all people who use antidepressants have side effects during the first few weeks of treatment. These problems are usually mild and don't last long.

Side effects of antidepressants may include:
- nervousness (usually temporary and may be relieved by decreasing the dose)
- nausea (temporary and usually occurs right after the dose is taken)
- a dry mouth (chew sugarless gum and drink lots of water)
- diarrhea (temporary, but drink lots of fluids to prevent dehydration)
- sleep problems (usually temporary and may be relieved by decreasing the dose)
- headaches (temporary)
- allergic reactions (these are rare)

The side effects will probably decrease once your body adjusts to the medication, but report *any* reactions to your mental health

*For more information about brain chemicals, see pages 34–36.

professional right away, especially if they're severe enough to make you afraid to continue taking your medication. You may be tempted to skip a dose or throw out your medication even if your side effects are mild; instead, report your symptoms to your mental health professional, who may ask you to continue the medication as prescribed and keep a record of any reactions you have. Write down the reactions in a journal or notebook that you can bring to your next appointment, and then tell your mental health professional about what's happening. Ask if it's possible to decrease the dose or take it at a different time of day to relieve the side effects. It's important to report *any* unexpected side effects, as well as feelings of hopelessness or anxiety, to your health care professional.

What About Herbal Remedies?

You may have heard about herbal remedies for depression—maybe you've even wondered if this kind of treatment could help you. In some countries, an herbal extract called St. John's wort may be prescribed for mild forms of depression, but in the United States, no scientific studies have proven that St. John's wort or any other herbal remedies are safe or effective. In fact, herbal remedies like St. John's wort could interact with other medications you may take, putting your health at risk. If you plan to use any kind of medication, even one that's considered "natural," you should do so only if a doctor or mental health professional has advised it. Discuss your options with an expert, so you have all the facts.

If you have bipolar disorder,* you'll need special medications because the illness has two phases—depression and mania. Your mental health professional can help you decide which type of antidepressant might help relieve your depressive symptoms (anxiety, sadness, hopelessness,

---

*For more information about bipolar disorder, see pages 24–27.

etc.). You'll also need to treat the manic symptoms of bipolar disorder (irritability, distraction, and racing thoughts, for example).

Medications used to treat the manic phase of bipolar illness are called mood stabilizers. If you start taking one of these medications, you'll need blood tests to determine whether your dosage is too high or low (too much can be harmful; too little won't help you). Once your doctor finds the amount that's right for you, you'll need to take the medication every day in regularly spaced doses to keep a constant amount in your blood.

The medications for bipolar disorder typically take a while to become effective, and they have more potential for side effects. This is why your mental health professional must monitor you on a regular basis. Some of the side effects may include nausea, weight gain, tremor, drowsiness, dizziness, headache, anxiety, or confusion. You will most likely not experience *all* of these effects, and those you do should be reported to your doctor immediately.

So, why would you want to take a medication that may cause uncomfortable side effects? Because the episodes of mania and depression are often severe, painful, and potentially life-altering. According to the Centers for Disease Control and Prevention, the suicide risk for people with bipolar disorder is more than twenty times higher than the general population, especially for those who don't receive treatment. *And, once you adjust to your medication, you'll begin to feel better and your moods will even out.* You shouldn't stop taking the medication once you feel better, however. Continue taking it just as prescribed and report any side effects to your mental health professional.

NOTE: If you're a teen taking an antidepressant or a mood stabilizer for bipolar disorder, you may have a negative reaction if you drink alcohol or take any other kind of drug, including over-the-counter medications, so be careful. (Ask your mental health professional about medications that may interact with your prescription.) Definitely avoid illegal drugs, including pot. If you *do* drink alcohol or take drugs, get in touch with your doctor to find out what you need to do to take care of yourself.

No matter what kind of depression medications you take, you may need to wait about four to six weeks before you'll feel their full benefit. Why so long? As Marcia Bentley, a psychiatric nurse practitioner, explains: "It's like the neurotransmitters in your brain have been hibernating like bears and are slow to wake up. The medication has to build up to a level where it actually begins to relieve your symptoms. That takes some time." If you've been feeling depressed for months or years, four to six weeks may not seem long in comparison.

If the medication doesn't seem to be working after six weeks, talk to your mental health professional. You might need to have it "boosted" by another medication, or you may have to switch to a different type. You'll eventually find a medication that's right for you.

You may worry about taking medication, especially if you think it might change your personality. Antidepressants may make you feel different, especially while your body adjusts, but you'll still be yourself. You'll have the same sense of humor, intelligence, and talents, plus a better outlook on life. You'll feel better, and your behavior will probably improve.

Antidepressants aren't habit-forming, so don't worry about getting addicted to them. You do have to be careful when taking these medications, though. *Never* mix any other medications—such as other prescriptions, over-the-counter medicines, or alcohol/drugs—without talking to your mental health professional first. And be sure not to stop taking doctor-prescribed medications on your own (this could lead to withdrawal symptoms and isn't safe to do).

Make a Schedule

Because depression can cause problems with your concentration and memory, you'll need a medication schedule that you can follow easily. Talk to your mental health professional about the amount of medication you need and when you should take it. Then make a schedule and post it in your room, on the refrigerator, or any other place where you'll see it each day. Ask a parent or caregiver to help you remember to take your medications while you get used to your schedule.

If you miss a dose, don't double the dosage the next time you take your medication (unless your mental health professional says it's okay to do this). Doubling a dose could cause a serious reaction.

Many schools have policies about medication, so look in your school handbook or ask your school nurse (if you have one) about it. You'll probably need to bring a note from a parent, indicating the times and reasons for taking your medication, if you take it during the day. You may have to store your medication at the nurse's office instead of carrying it with you. If your school doesn't have a nurse on staff, talk to your principal about your situation and find out if the school has rules about a teacher or an aide administering medication.

Shawnelle's Story

Shawnelle's long-term sadness and anger eventually led to depression. Over the years, she tried many forms of treatment, including sharing her feelings with a weekly group at school, seeing a psychiatrist, and taking anti-depressants. After several suicide attempts, Shawnelle went to an Adolescent Treatment Unit (ATU) where she finally learned to deal with her feelings and set goals for herself. Although she experienced several setbacks throughout her years of trying to get treatment, Shawnelle eventually overcame her depression.

I think I've always been sad, but I didn't know it was a problem. I was never allowed to express anger as a child, so I learned to hold it inside. As I grew, my anger grew. I was unhappy in junior high, and by the time I was sixteen, I generally felt sad, hopeless, and angry.

That year, a group of Russian students came to our school as part of a foreign exchange program, and they became a part of my life. I made friends with them, studied with them, and even learned a Russian dance. I spent a lot of time with one of the girls, Masha, and we grew quite close. She was surprised that I could be sad and depressed when I "had so much" and "lived in such a great country." For the nearly two months the Russian students stayed in the United States, I felt better than I had in a long time.

When the Russian students left at the end of the school year, depression hit me full force again. I was involved with a group of kids who met once a week at school to talk about family problems; the group was facilitated by a drug and alcohol counselor whom I had come to trust. When I told her about my sadness and that I had headaches and trouble sleeping, she suggested I see a doctor. I was afraid to tell the doctor about feeling sad most of the time because I didn't want to be diagnosed as depressed. I didn't want to feel so bad all the time either, so I admitted everything, and the doctor prescribed an antidepressant.

For a long time, I was still in a lot of pain. When I was discovered in the bathroom at school, crying and pulling my hair, my group counselor thought I was suicidal. She arranged for me to be evaluated at an emergency room, where I was voluntarily admitted to the hospital's mental health unit. I attended group therapy sessions, learned about setting goals for myself, talked with the staff about some of the problems I was having, and saw the psychiatrist daily. He increased the dosage of my antidepressant. I was there a week, felt better, and went home on Easter Sunday to spend the holiday with my family.

Eight days after I left the hospital, I had another setback, and I realized I needed to go somewhere with a strong program for young people with problems like mine. I went to the Adolescent Treatment Unit in my community. During the orientation period, I had to start with the basics: I wore a sweatsuit provided for me instead of my own clothes, and my shoes and shoelaces were taken away. I couldn't go outside or have visitors, either. I was allowed to receive phone calls only from my mom and therapist. I had to earn privileges by completing certain tasks and participating in groups and activities.

I eventually discovered that my biggest issue was anger. All my anger caused a lot of pain, which led to depression. I expressed my anger by being mean, stubborn, and uncooperative, and by hurting myself. Slowly, though, I began to feel safe talking about things that made me angry. I learned that anger is a normal emotion that needs to be let out in safe ways, not swallowed down where it can fester and grow.

"When you feel sad, look for the reason and try to put it in perspective. You can discuss your feelings with a counselor, a friend, or someone else you trust. Crying can take the pressure off, too." —Shawnelle

I received a letter from Masha, reminding me that I would soon be visiting Russia as part of my school's foreign-exchange program. She said she was looking forward to seeing me. Her letter helped motivate me to get my act together and finish my work at the ATU. I helped plan my discharge date, how I was going to deal with my feelings in the real world before they became overwhelming, and whom I would talk with on a regular basis.

In September of 1996, I went to Russia. It was wonderful to see all my friends and to meet new ones. I wrote a poem while I was there—a poem about how it feels to finally be free of the terrible burden of depression.

Past Me, Present

Can you imagine me so happy I could fly?
Melancholy me, smile upon my face,
laughter flowing out
for the whole world to hear.
I'm back.
Normal once more.

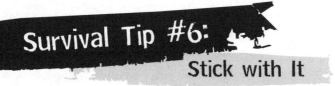

Survival Tip #6:
Stick with It

*"**Strength is a matter of the made-up mind.**"* —John Beecher

Whether you're in therapy, on medication, or both, sticking with your treatment plan is the single most important thing you can do to get better and stay well. Not following your treatment plan is like refusing to paddle your raft anymore when you know a waterfall is around the next bend.

Make a commitment to follow your treatment plan for a certain length of time—for example, four weeks. During this time, keep in touch with your mental health professional, who can help you adjust the plan as needed. Once you reach the four-week milestone, commit to another four weeks of treatment. Setting and reaching goals will help you feel more in control of your treatment and your life.

Ways to stick with your treatment:

- Use a calendar or day planner to record your therapy or doctor appointments, so you don't forget them.

- If you're taking medication, make a schedule. For added help, put a reminder note on the bathroom mirror or in another place where you'll see it each day.

- Keep a piece of paper handy, so you can write down any questions or concerns as you think of them. Store your notes in your wallet, pocket, or notebook, or tape them somewhere at home or in your locker. Bring the questions along when you see your therapist.

Chart Your Moods

When you're recovering from depression, you may improve slowly, and sometimes it's hard to notice you're getting better. By charting your moods each day, you can see your recovery on paper. A Mood Chart is a great way to keep track of your good days and bad days, and to see what triggers your emotions.

The chart will also be a helpful tool for your mental health professional, who can use it to see if your treatment is helping. Bring it to each appointment, so your caregiver can review what's been going on since your last visit. You can photocopy the chart on pages 110–111 or make your own.

Here's how you fill out a Mood Chart:

1. The numbers across the top stand for the days of the month, so first find the day you're starting. You'll use that numbered column to record your mood.

2. Choose a time at the end of the day to write on the chart and try to stick to that schedule.

3. Record what your mood was for most of the day (fill in one square only). The mood descriptions along the side of the chart range from really high to really low, and somewhere in between. If you felt good for most of the day, put a mark (a dot, a check, an X, or whatever) in the "Good" box. If you felt just so-so, mark the "Fair" box. If your emotions fell somewhere in the middle, mark the square between "Good" and "Fair." If you felt really terrible, fill out "In the Gutter." (Note: If you have more than two or three days of "In the Gutter" or "Above the Clouds," let your mental health professional know.) Filling out your mood chart is kind of like connecting the dots. You'll soon see your progress for an entire month.

On the lower part of the chart is a section called "Big Deal of the Day." This is your comment section, where you can write a few words about any significant event that occurred that day. You could record a good grade you got, a compliment someone gave you, or a funny thing that happened. Or you could write about something that upset you—a fight with a friend or a bad grade, for example. This is also a good place to note any side effects, changes in your medication, or new symptoms you might be having. You don't have to limit yourself to just one event, if you don't want to; because there's not a lot of space, you might just jot down a few key words, then go into more detail in your journal. The Big Deal of the Day sections can remind you of how stressors in your life affect your moods and will show you which emotional issues you may need help with.

You can tape your completed charts on a wall side-by-side to watch your moods improve. But don't expect the line to move steadily upward—recovery from depression is an up-and-down process, and it takes time to get better.

Mood Chart

My mood for most of each day
in the month of: _____

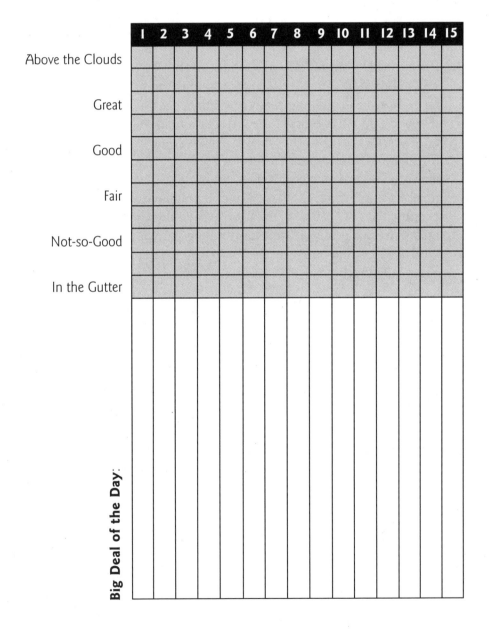

	1	2	3	4	5	6	7	8	9	10	11	12	13	14	15
Above the Clouds															
Great															
Good															
Fair															
Not-so-Good															
In the Gutter															
Big Deal of the Day:															

110

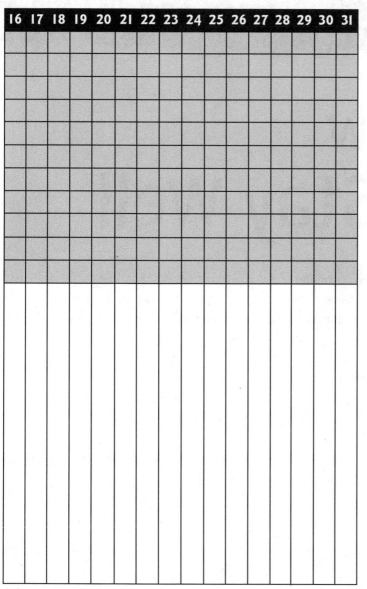

16	17	18	19	20	21	22	23	24	25	26	27	28	29	30	31

7

"I'm sitting and watching a butterfly. It's like I'm waking up from a long sleep." —Ernie, 17

How to Stay Well

Once you've recovered from most of the symptoms of depression and are thinking more clearly, you'll want to work on staying well. One way to stay well is to understand that *you* are in charge of helping yourself to be healthy. *You* make the ultimate decisions.

It's up to you to decide to:
- follow the seven Survival Tips (listed throughout this book)
- make the positive changes that will improve your life

No one can do these things for you. If you get discouraged, talk to someone. Getting and staying well takes time and hard work, but it's worth the effort.

Ideas for Staying Strong

- Be patient with yourself when you feel tired, sad, or irritable in the early stages of your treatment. Your symptoms may not go away for several weeks or more. Treat yourself as you would your best friend (with care and respect).

- Ask your family and friends if they see a difference in your behavior and outlook. Sometimes you may not think you're getting better when you really are.

- Don't stop or change any part of your treatment without first talking about your decision with your family and your mental health professional. Ask for their advice and support.

- Put off any big decisions or new projects until you're feeling better. You have enough to deal with right now.

- Be sure your home environment feels safe and nurturing. If it doesn't, you may need to seek family counseling or move away from home temporarily until you're feeling better (a caring relative or friend's family may be willing to take you in for a while).

- Keep a journal of your feelings, activities, experiences, goals, and successes. A journal is a safe place for exploring your feelings through writing, art, poetry, or doodling. Whatever you put in your journal is private, and no one else needs to see it. Reviewing your journal is a good way to tell if your thinking is negative or positive.

Staying Positive

To stay positive, be aware of how your mind and body work together. Your thoughts influence your physical, mental, and emotional self in very dramatic ways. Part of staying well is learning to think positive and control your thoughts.

Say you're feeling lost in class one day at school. How do you react? If you think angry, negative thoughts like "I'm so stupid; I'll never pass this class," your *thoughts* of anger will lead to feelings of anger, which in turn will lead to *physical expressions* of anger (a scowl, a rise in blood pressure, a faster heartbeat). Your body, mind, and emotions are all working together to make you feel angry.

You're in charge of what you *think* about an event, and therefore how you *feel* about it, and ultimately how you *react* to it. Because your thoughts are very powerful, you can learn to change how you feel by changing the way you think. Finding healthy new ways to control your feelings can keep your depression from returning.

Many teens who recover from depression don't want to face the fact that it could come back again. Once you're well, staying well is something you'll need to work on every day. Watch for any signs of a relapse—new symptoms, painful feelings, and negative thoughts. The earlier you catch the symptoms, the sooner you can tell someone, get help, and recover again.

Getting On with Your Life

John, a depressed teen at a hospital mental health unit, was going through treatment and had started feeling better. In the few days he'd been at the hospital, only his parents and minister had visited him. When asked why no friends had come by, John said, "None of my friends know I'm here. They wouldn't understand. I'm afraid they might not want to be my friends anymore if they knew." Then John thought about what would happen if his best friend seemed sad or disturbed for a while, and then suddenly stopped coming to school. He knew that he'd feel concerned about his friend and would want to help. This prompted John to call his closest friend, Jay, and explain what he'd been going through. Jay arrived at the unit within twenty minutes, and the two boys talked. Their friendship survived—and perhaps became even stronger.

You don't have to feel ashamed or embarrassed about your depression or treatment. At first, it may be a little uncomfortable to tell your friends what's been going on in your life. If you've been isolated for a while, you may feel awkward about calling people on the phone or spending time with your friends again. Trust that your friends won't judge you; they care about you and want you to feel good. Following are some ideas for telling your friends what's been happening.

You Can Say:

- "I'm glad I have friends like you to talk to about what's been going on with me. The past few weeks (months) have been really hard because I've been depressed. I'm getting better, though, and I could use your support."

- "I know I've been out of it socially for a while, but I'm feeling more like myself again, so feel free to ask me anything you want. It will help me to talk about what I've been going through."

- "Depression had me feeling pretty down for a while. It was difficult to accept that I needed help, but now I'm starting to feel better. I have to be careful to take good care of myself so that I can get even stronger and stay that way."

- "I still need to take it slow, but I'm getting back to my usual self again. It won't embarrass me to talk about what I've been through, so if there's anything you want to know, just ask."

- "It was helpful for me to learn that millions of people go through depression, and now I'm finally over the worst of it. I'm glad you've stuck by me. Depression is nothing to be ashamed of, so go ahead and ask me about it."

- "Ta-da! I'm back, you lucky people, and I'm better than ever! You'll notice that I will now be taking better care of myself, and you can help me do that by encouraging me to share my feelings and by letting me know if you see me sinking down again."

It may be helpful to give your friends some brochures about depression so they can read about what happens and how to cope. You can get free brochures and fact sheets from the national organizations listed on page 134.

Sometimes friends and classmates may not know what to say when you start feeling better and are ready to be social again. They may be afraid of hurting your feelings or embarrassing you. In most cases, you'll find that as soon as you let your friends know that you want to talk about what's been happening to you, they'll help you as much as they can. In fact, they'll probably feel relieved to know they aren't the only ones having problems coping with being a teen. Getting through difficult times together usually brings friends closer.

TIP: You've probably heard this before, but if your friends drop you when you need them most, they're not your friends. Think about how you'd react if a friend was going through what you've been through—you'd probably want to help any way you could. If someone snubs you or makes fun of you when you talk about your depression, you don't need that person in your life. People who really care about you will understand. Focus on strengthening the friendships that truly matter.

Dealing with School

If you've missed school because of your depression, talk to your principal and teachers about your situation and ask them if they can help you find ways to catch up. It may help to bring a family adult along for this conversation, so you have extra support.

You Can Say:

- "You probably know that I've been absent for a while because I was depressed. I'm being treated for my depression, and I'm getting better. I'd be grateful for your help and support while I'm getting well."

- "As you know, I've missed class lately, but I really want to catch up. Is it possible for me to make up some of my work or try some extra-credit assignments?"

- "Now that I'm back at school and feeling better, I'd like to bring my grade up. Could you help me find a tutor or work with me one-on-one, so I can catch up?"

- "I'm on medication for depression, so sometimes I might be a little drowsy in class. Please don't think that I'm bored or not trying. Once I adjust to the medication, I'll be able to focus once again."

- "Do you think I might have to explore summer school options? I know I've missed some class and I'm behind—can you help me figure out what I need to do?"

▪ "Thanks for being patient and understanding while I'm getting well. If you think I might be falling into a depression again, let me know. Don't be afraid to talk to me about any symptoms you might see."

If your principal and teachers don't know much about depression, give them pamphlets or fact sheets (you can get these free materials from the national organizations listed on page 134).

Helping Others Help You

One of the most important things you, your family, and your friends can do to help you recover is to understand that depression isn't shameful. You don't have to feel guilty about being depressed. The more you talk about depression openly and honestly with people you trust, the more acceptable the topic becomes. You can do your part to help others talk about depression, recognize it, and treat it. Learn all you can about your depression and teach others what you know.

Another way your family and friends can help you is by noticing how you're changing, even in small ways. Ask the people who care about you to tell you when they notice any positive differences in your appearance or behavior. It may take a while for you to start feeling your best, and you may not be aware that you're paying more attention to your appearance, showing up for class more often, smiling more, spending less time in your room, or eating a little more (or less). Your brain and body heal from depression a little at a time, not overnight. Remind your loved ones that you need their care and support.

It's wonderful to have support from the people who care about you, but the person who can help you the most is you. You need to be your own best friend now, so treat yourself with gentleness, care, and respect. Make good decisions for yourself. Learn to feel good about who you are and what you can do. Get up every morning and choose to be well.

Tyler's Story

In addition to seeing a counselor for his depression, Tyler also uses a kind of therapy he created for himself—it's called Leak Therapy, or Leaking. This way, Tyler is able to let out his negative feelings little by little in creative and healthy ways.

I see a counselor for my depression, but I've learned to keep my feelings under control by Leaking. Leaking is something I devised on my own; I guess you could call it Leak Therapy. I've learned to deal with pressure by putting the "inside" things out there instead of holding them in until I just fly into a rage. It's like letting a little air out of a raft. I'm constantly leaking air out of the valve—I keep just the right amount of air in the raft to keep it afloat, but not enough to burst it.

I'm always letting stuff leak out, even when I don't feel bad. I listen to "thrash" music; I paint on the walls of my room, using wild, grungy colors; and I've recently started doing self-portraits on canvas board. Drawing is a big way that I leak. I rarely get mad anymore because I let my feelings leak out in very expressive, but safe, ways.

When I was depressed, I would let myself think about how I was messing up in school and other things, and I'd just crumple up into a ball on my bed. My insides would churn and squirm. I didn't know what to do or how to think about what was happening. I wanted to escape—to press a button and be out of my body. I didn't want to feel. When I got angry, I either exploded or walked away. Counseling finally helped me. I talked about all the things that bothered me, and every week, I let more feelings leak out. The more I talked to the counselor, the more I could organize my thinking. It was good for me.

At home, doing laundry and other housework became a leak. I took resentments out on the laundry by throwing the socks into the washer as hard as I could and by snapping the towels in the air. Taking out the trash was a leak—I stomped it down into the can. My other leaks are listening to music, painting, drawing, writing, and turning my bedroom into a work of art. I live in my art—even the jeans I wear are art (I made them from many pieces of denim, and my friend calls them my "dramatic britches"). All of this is working for me.

> "I believe we find our own answers to our problems, but sometimes we just need help asking the right questions. You'll eventually find what works for you." —Tyler

The new emerging me, the me right now, is very mellow. I don't have blasting anger, and I don't feel depressed.

Survival Tip #7:
Feed Your Spirit

"I've always believed that you can think positive just as well as you can think negative." —Sugar Ray Robinson

Overcoming depression is a matter of healing your physical and emotional self, but another part of you may be damaged, too—your personal spirit. When you're depressed, a place inside you feels empty. This place, which holds your personal spirit, needs attention.

Feeding your spirit is like having your own personal pep rally—where you shout "Hurray for me!" You need to feel proud of who you are and what you're trying to do. You need to want yourself to win.

Instead of yelling *at* yourself, yell *for* yourself. Show compassion for yourself when you make a mistake. Pat yourself on the back when you succeed at something. Realize that you may have a bad day once in a while, but you can get through it and move on.

Ways to feed your personal spirit:

- Write your thoughts and feelings in a journal. Don't edit what you write—you don't have to show it to anyone.

- Listen to music you love. Dance or move to the music. If you play a musical instrument or sing, make up a song. (Singing songs you love adds joy to your day. And movement is good for gathering energy and feeding your spirit.)

- Write a poem, short story, or any other creative piece.

- Walk on the beach and listen to the waves and birds, or take a long walk through a forest or park. Hug a tree. (Come on, try it!) If you don't live near a beach or forest, walk someplace else that feels peaceful.

- Volunteer your time at your local Red Cross, a senior center, an animal shelter, or an environmental organization. Helping others or doing good is a great way to help yourself.

- Collect something you love. Think of a unique way to display your collection.

- Go to an art gallery or a museum and spend time looking at the paintings and sculptures.

- Paint, draw, or sketch a picture. Make a collage or a sculpture with found objects.

- Be creative in any way you like. Use a needle and thread, paper, ink, flowers, music, cloth, words, glue, or wood. Borrow ideas from magazines, other people, art books, hobby shops, or nature. See what's inside you, waiting to come out.

- Spend time with an animal friend. Petting a dog or watching fish swim around can make you feel very peaceful. If you don't have a pet, spend time with a neighbor's pet or visit an animal shelter to volunteer your time.

- Buy a plant that's easy to care for, put it in your room, and watch it grow.

- If you're comfortable with praying, say a prayer.

- Because you want good friends, *be* a good friend.

- Make cookies or a meal for someone who has been kind to you.

- Join a support group and go at least once a week.

- Learn everything you can about depression and your treatment. Become an expert about your own depression so you know how to get better.

- Set a goal to do something you've always wanted to do. Plan it out in simple steps, write them down, and do step number one. After you've completed one step, you'll have the confidence to tackle the next step.

Top Ten Questions

Since the first version of *When Nothing Matters Anymore* was published, I have heard from hundreds of teens from all over the world, asking questions about their situations. Even though some of the answers to their questions were addressed in the book, they seemed to need a more personal touch, recognition, or perhaps reassurance that their problems really did have solutions. Because of these teens, I have chosen ten of the most frequently asked questions I've received and then answered them here. In this section, you'll find references to pages throughout this book so you can find additional information on these topics.

I believe that an unanswered question is a problem unsolved, so if you have other questions that aren't listed here, please don't be afraid to find a trusted adult and ask. *Talking helps.* To give you an example from my own life, I recently became overwhelmed with many situations that were causing me stress. I wasn't sleeping well, and I felt like crying all the time. I was worried that I would become depressed again, even though I continue to take an antidepressant. Finally, I realized that I needed to talk to someone I trusted—someone who could think clearly—and I went to see a good friend. Within an hour, she had helped me find another perspective and reset my priorities. I left her home feeling a new bounce in my step, and I have since been able to think more clearly, take care of my situation, and reduce my stress level. Talking to someone—a friend, a parent, or a teacher—is a way to take care of yourself.

As you read this section, keep in mind that there is rarely just one right answer for everyone. Keep asking until you find *your* answers.

Q & A

1. If I feel sad a lot, does it mean I'm depressed?
Not necessarily. Young people have a lot of stress to deal with: school, sports/activities, jobs, changing bodies, worries about how they look,

questions about the future, and sometimes family problems or even abuse. If your sadness is affecting your life to the point that you find it terribly difficult to interact with others or can't function the way you want to or used to, then this may be the beginning of depression. The sooner you find out, the sooner you can do something to feel better. See a doctor to find out what's going on with you. If you know why you're feeling sad, talking with an understanding, trusted adult can help change the way you feel. Think about who you might go to. For more help, see pages 92–93.

2. Does being depressed mean I'm crazy?

Absolutely not. Depression is an illness that affects your brain and body. You can learn about how depression affects the brain (see Chapter 3), and you can read descriptions of the physical/emotional symptoms of depression (see Chapter 2). There are treatments for depression, just as there are treatments for other medical illnesses.

3. Do I have to take medications to feel better if I'm depressed?

If you've been diagnosed by a psychiatrist who specializes in treating adolescents and who believes you're depressed, medications are an option for helping you feel better faster. The psychiatrist who diagnoses you will probably have suggestions for treatment, which may include a combination of medication and therapy. Some teens are afraid that medications for depression are addictive or will change their personality, but when used properly, these medications are designed to help you to be a "better feeling *you*." You'll still be the same person, but you'll be taking care of your illness under the care of an expert who can see how the medication affects you. Studies show that a combination of medication and talking with a therapist is, for most people, the fastest way to feel better. See Chapter 6 for more on medications and therapy.

4. I think one of my friends may be depressed. How can I help?

Talking with your friend about the way he or she feels and being nonjudgmental is a good start. Ask questions, instead of giving advice. You may want to say something like, "I can see that you're hurting, do you want to talk about it?" or "Is there anything I can do to help you feel better?" If your friend talks about feeling hopeless or doesn't improve in a few days, it's best to turn the problem over to an adult who can help, such as a teacher, a school nurse, a school counselor, your friend's parent, or someone else you trust. By getting help from an adult, you're taking a step toward keeping your friend safer and healthier. If your friend ever mentions thoughts of suicide or wishing to die, get help from an adult *right away*. You'll find a list of hotlines on pages 82.

5. Sometimes I feel like others expect too much of me. I'm starting to worry all the time. Help.
Too much worrying is unhealthy. No one can please everyone—it's impossible! If your family and friends seem to have unrealistic expectations for you, talk to them about how you feel. Let them know that, like anyone else, you have your limits. You might make a list of all the things you worry about, and then talk to the people in your life who seem to expect too much of you. Share your list with them and work together to set some more realistic priorities and goals. You can also talk with an adult you trust at school.

You might find it helpful to read all of the Survival Tips at the end of each chapter. Every tip provides ideas for getting and staying healthy, not just mentally but physically, too. The tips can help you feel stronger and more balanced—which may help you to keep your worries at bay.

6. My best friend recently moved away, and I'm feeling depressed. Why can't I just get over it?
It sounds as if you're grieving the loss of someone you care about. That person isn't in your life every day anymore, and that hurts. Grief is a natural response to loss. You may find it helpful to read books about grief and let yourself cry or be angry and sad when those feelings come up. Write in a journal and take long walks. *Feel* your feelings, instead of telling yourself you have to get over them.

Reaching out to other friends and talking about your loss is another good way to work through the grief process. If you don't start feeling better within a few weeks or if you begin to withdraw from your other friends, try seeking support from a professional or a local support group that focuses on coping with grief. Talking to the adults in your family may help, too.

7. I think I have poor self-esteem. I feel I don't do anything right.
Everyone feels this way at times. You can make a list of the things that you know you do well—everyone is good at *something*. Maybe you write poems, play an instrument, are a good listener, or take great care of your pet. Pick something you do well and work to do it even better. This will help build your confidence.

Your thoughts are powerful. Tell yourself *good* things about yourself, instead of trying to find flaws. Ask friends and family members to point out your good points. Write their positive words in your journal so you can look at them when you feel down. Most of all, believe that you're a good person. No one is perfect—and you don't have to be either.

P.S. A great way to feel better about yourself is to help others. You can volunteer at an organization in your community or look for service projects at your school. If this sounds difficult for you right now, start small. Help out a neighbor or a family member. Let those positive feelings motivate you to do more good things for others.

8. I am overweight, and other people stare at me and call me names. I'm sick of it. I get depressed when people act this way.
Decide how you want to look and take action. If you're comfortable with your appearance, tell people so and keep working on accepting yourself. Ignore the stares and comments, and focus on the positive things in your life (like family and friends who value you for who you are). This isn't only about your appearance, though—it's about your health. Take an honest look at your weight, your eating habits, and your level of physical activity. Does something need to change? See a doctor to get accurate information about what a healthy weight is for someone of your body type and age. If you want to lose weight, make a decision to do so. Change your eating habits slowly and start an exercise program, with the help of a doctor. Eating right and exercising regularly can help fend off some of the symptoms of depression. For more about the importance of staying active and eating healthy foods, see Survival Tip #1 and Survival Tip #4 (pages 15–17 and 68–72).

9. I'm often overwhelmed with things going on in my life: school, family, relationships, and so on. What can I do when I'm anxious?
Most teens have daily stress and temporary feelings of being overwhelmed. That's normal, especially when you have a busy school schedule, an after-school job, extracurricular activities, and other commitments. All that juggling can leave you feeling anxious. But sometimes, feelings of being overwhelmed aren't temporary—they last throughout the day and seem to overtake your life. Is this what's happening to you? See the quiz on page 11, which can help you take a deeper look at your feelings and figure out if you may have some symptoms of depression. You may want to show the results of the quiz to a parent, a doctor, or a trusted adult at school.

If you find that your anxious feelings come and go, try some deep breathing when you start to feel stressed. Breathe in through your nose for a count of five; breathe out slowly through your mouth, counting backwards from five. Repeat this several times and see if you begin to calm down. You can also try a relaxation exercise—there's a good one on pages 32–33. You may also want to increase your physical activity to make sure you have a release for your tension. Avoid caffeine, since it increases adrenaline and can make you feel more anxious. Look for other ways to stay calm (try yoga, journal writing, and talking to friends).

10. My parents think I need to go to a treatment center because I drink alcohol and smoke marijuana. I don't like to talk about myself and don't think treatment can help me. What do you think?
When people abuse or become addicted to alcohol or other drugs, the chemicals take over their minds and bodies. Treatment doesn't mean you're a "failure" or a "bad" person—treatment means you're getting help for problems that are too big to handle on your own.

Substance abuse or addictions most often lead to further problems, like depression, illness, or an accident. And that's why it's so important to get help. In a treatment center, you'll be with other teens who are dealing with the same issues you are. You'll see that you aren't alone. Most people I know who go for treatment come out feeling healthier and happier about themselves; they also gain new coping skills so that they can live well without drugs and alcohol. In other words, I agree with your parents—treatment can help you. It can help improve your life if you just give it a chance. For more on this topic, see Chapter 4.

A Final Word

I recently received an email from a mom whose fourteen-year-old daughter, Jill, had read my book in a health class and realized that the feelings of sadness and loneliness she had been struggling with for so long might be the result of depression. Hesitant to talk about her situation, Jill decided to write her feelings and thoughts in a letter, which she gave to her mom one morning just before running out the door to catch the bus. Jill's mom had noticed that her daughter seemed "different" lately but thought she was just going through a normal teen phase. In her email to me, Jill's mom thanked me for helping her daughter find a way to reach out for the help she needed.

I know that many teens have trouble expressing their pain to adults who could help them, perhaps because of embarrassment, confusion, and the fear that they might not be taken seriously. For some teens, writing about their struggles may be an easier way to reach out to a parent or another adult. If you want to write a letter asking for help, you can use the sample one on page 128 as a start. Adapt it to fit your situation—change whatever will make the letter more meaningful for you. A letter can be a safe way to get the support you need. Please ask for help so you don't have to keep struggling on your own.

Dear _____ ,

I'm having a difficult time in my life right now, and I don't know what to do to change things. I hope this letter will help you understand me better. I have so many feelings that hurt. At times, I feel like no one cares about me. I feel lonely and sad. I know I do things that upset you, and I don't like that either. I'm so confused. I think I may even be depressed. I know I need help, but I'm afraid to ask for it. I'm worried that you might not take me seriously. I am serious, though. Please help me.

Sincerely,

_____

Can Anything Good Come of This?

If you've had problems, difficulties, or illness in your life (and who hasn't?), at some point along the way you've probably asked the question "Why me?" Maybe the answer you got was that difficulties in life are "learning experiences." Did you believe it?

No one is immune to tragedy, bad luck, or ill fate. But everyone can learn to stand strong against hardship and adversity. Don't let depression get the best of you. You can survive physically, emotionally, and spiritually.

Sometimes problems may even be gifts in disguise. Have you ever heard the story about the man whose only riches were his beloved son and his twenty stallions?

> One night, the corral gate was left open, and the man's twenty stallions ran away into the hills. The man wept and cursed his bad luck. The next morning, he awoke to find that his twenty stallions had returned, each with a wild mare. "This is very good, for now I have forty horses," he said. But his beloved son was thrown while trying to ride one of the wild mares, and he broke his leg in the accident. "How horrible!" cried the man. "My son is in such pain. This is very bad!" That evening, a hundred of the king's soldiers swept through the village and gathered all the able-bodied young men to fight a war far away. The man's son wasn't taken because of his broken leg. The man laughed and said to his son, "Perhaps, in this case, a broken leg is good."

Sometimes how you think about an event and how you react to it are more important than the event itself. If something happens that you don't like, you can *choose* how to deal with it.

If you look at your misfortunes as learning experiences and life challenges that you can survive and overcome, you'll grow stronger.

Ask yourself, "How can I make this work *for* me instead of against me?" Tell yourself you won't just be a victim of your circumstances—you'll accept them, deal with them . . . and rise above them.

If you have depression, you can make it your responsibility to learn how to get well—and stay well. Depression offers you an opportunity to learn powerful new ways of taking care of your health and coping with life's challenges. You'll begin to develop character, endurance, and patience, and you'll understand how to take good care of yourself for the rest of your life. Learning how to survive depression can actually help make you a happier and healthier person.

"Character cannot be developed in ease and quiet. Only through experience of trial and suffering can the soul be strengthened, vision cleared, ambition inspired, and success achieved." —Helen Keller

A Note to Parents

by Elizabeth McCauley, Ph.D.

Dear Parents,

As we shoulder the responsibilities of adult life, many of us look back at adolescence as a carefree time—somehow forgetting the difficult struggles the teen years held. Some idealize this period as "the best years of your life," while others minimize adolescent concerns with a "What do *you* have to worry about?" attitude. This book serves as an important reminder that teens struggle with very real and serious issues.

It's important for parents of teens to try to understand what it's like to walk in their shoes. As Bev Cobain states in this book, "Being a teen is a hard job." Teens face changes and challenges in every aspect of their lives—as their bodies change so do the expectations of parents, teachers, and even friends. Adolescents must invent and reinvent themselves in their quest to fit in and find acceptance, while also working to figure out who they are and how to express their individuality.

Teens have a unique cognitive style—they see the world through fresh eyes. What they feel and experience may be age-old, but each adolescent feels at times like he or she is the first to experience feeling so intensely happy, sad, or alone, or to be so full of ideas. This intensity of feeling is frequently coupled with a tendency to view the world, and themselves, through an all-or-nothing lens: They are "popular" or "unpopular," things are "good" or "bad," life looks "wonderful" or "hopeless." This worldview modulates over the course of normal adolescent development, but in its most active phase, it places young people at particular risk for depression.

A teen's internal struggles are compounded by having to cope with the many other stressors that are part and parcel of life for an adolescent today—family problems and pressures, violence in communities and schools, drug and alcohol exposure, and the complexity of

131

the modern world. All of these stressors make it hard to develop a clear and positive sense of self, solid values, and goals for the future. The economic and social demands on today's parents frequently mean less family time and more pressure on youth to either be superstars or to simply get by on their own. These are difficult times for both parents and teens.

It's not easy to guide your child through adolescence, and the challenge becomes even greater when your child is coping with depression. You may become frustrated, even angry, when your child is moody and withdrawn, and rejects your every effort to help. This book serves as an excellent guide for navigating these difficult, and sometimes treacherous, waters—it reminds you that you're neither at fault nor alone. Depression happens to all kinds of adolescents—A students, star athletes, kids with family problems, and kids with loving and involved families. Teens who have depression didn't ask for it, and they certainly don't deserve it—and as a parent, neither do you. However, you can do your part to help your teen overcome depression. Communication is the first step.

The stories of the young people in this book provide an invaluable window into how teens feel and think. With this understanding, you can, as the book stresses, serve the tremendously important role of being a person your teen can talk to. Although you can't solve all of your child's problems, you can be a good listener—one who expresses concern, and most of all, reinforces the message "You can get better; we will find help."

I encourage you to use this book as a resource for yourself and your teen. It's full of timely, accurate information about depression, and provides a wealth of resources that you can call upon to find help and support for your teen and for yourself. Remember, for many adults, a lifelong struggle with depression begins during the teen years. Helping young people face, understand, and overcome depression may empower them with the skills they need to become happy, healthy, productive, and responsible adults.

You are your teen's most valuable ally in the fight to defeat depression. Depression is a *treatable* problem. You have every reason to feel hopeful about your teen's future.

Sincerely,

Elizabeth McCauley, Ph.D.
Professor, Department of Psychiatry and Behavioral Sciences
University of Washington
Chief, Adolescent Mental Health Clinic
Children's Hospital and Regional Medical Center
Seattle, Washington

Resources

National Organizations
Depression and Bipolar Support Alliance
730 North Franklin Street, Suite 501
Chicago, IL 60610
1-800-826-3632
This organization sends out free materials on the topic of depression and manic depression (bipolar disorder). Online: www.dbsalliance.org

The National Alliance on Mental Illness (NAMI)
Colonial Place Three
2107 Wilson Boulevard, Suite 300
Arlington, VA 22201
1-800-950-6264 (NAMI Information Helpline)
Even if you're not sure if you're depressed or why you're feeling a certain way, you can call the Information Helpline (Monday through Friday, between 10 A.M. and 6 P.M. EST). You will be greeted by an informative staff person who will talk with you, answer your questions, suggest resources, send information specifically for teens, and help you locate a self-help group in your area. Online: www.nami.org

National Institute of Mental Health (NIMH)
Public Information and Communications Branch
6001 Executive Boulevard, Room 8184, MSC 9663
Bethesda, MD 20892
1-866-615-6464
This program sends free information on depression and treatment for depressive disorders. You can request a number of brochures on specific topics. Online: www.nimh.nih.gov

Books

Depression Is the Pits, But I'm Getting Better: A Guide for Adolescents by E. Jane Garland, M.D. (Magination Press, 1998). This basic book explains teen depression, medications, counseling, and how to cope.

"Help Me, I'm Sad": Recognizing, Treating, and Preventing Childhood and Adolescent Depression by David G. Fassler, M.D., and Lynn S. Dumas (Penguin, 1998). Although this book was written for adults, it explains how parents can play a vital role in helping young people overcome depression. It includes information on spotting symptoms, preventing suicide, getting help, and choosing a treatment.

The Power to Prevent Suicide: A Guide for Teens Helping Teens by Richard E. Nelson, Ph.D., and Judith C. Galas (Free Spirit Publishing Inc., 2006). This practical guide explains the causes of suicide, how to recognize the warning signs, and how to reach out to save a life.

Web sites

Internet Mental Health
www.mentalhealth.com
Developed by Phillip W. Long, M.D., this award-winning site is designed to help anyone who has an interest in mental health, including teens. You'll find information and extensive links to other Web sites, including those on depression, eating disorders, substance abuse, and other mental health issues.

TeensHealth
www.kidshealth.org/teen
This site offers lots of great information on all aspects of health, including mental health. Information is specific to teens, so it's quick and easy to find facts important to you.

Endnotes

1. Art Buchwald, "Celebrity Meltdown: Famous, Important People Who Have Suffered Depression" *Psychology Today* (November 1999); "Famous People with Depression," About.com: http://depression.about.com/od/famous.

2. Results of a study by Dr. John Bartholomew, published in *Medicine & Science in Sports & Exercise,* Vol. 37:12 (January 2006).

3. Boris Birmaher, M.D., Neal D. Ryan, M.D., Douglas E. Williamson, B.A., David A. Brent, M.D., Joan Kaufman, Ph.D., Ronald E. Dahl, M.D., James Perel, Ph.D., and Beverly Nelson, R.N., "Childhood and Adolescent Depression: A Review of the Past 10 Years, Part I," *The Journal of the American Academy of Child and Adolescent Psychiatry,* Vol. 35:11 (November 1996).

4. Derek Burnett, "Safe at Home?" *Reader's Digest* (October 2005).

5. Luis H. Zayas, Ph.D., "Why Do So Many Latina Teens Attempt Suicide? A Conceptual Model for Research," *American Journal of Orthopsychiatry,* Vol. 75:2 (April 2005).

Index

137

About the Author

Bev Cobain is a Registered Nurse with National Accreditation in the psychiatric/mental health field. She practiced in several fields of nursing before she discovered her passion lay in the areas of drug/alcohol rehabilitation and mental health, where, on hospital-based units, she helped treat teens and adults. She is a nationally recognized speaker and workshop facilitator on issues of depression awareness, suicide prevention/intervention, and family healing following the death of a loved one to suicide. In 1999, Bev was honored with the "Green Ribbon," awarded by the National Mental Health Association in recognition of her efforts to help youth cope with depression.

Bev's own experiences of sexual abuse, panic disorder, alcoholism, major depression, and suicidality have helped her to understand the struggles of young people. Kurt Cobain's suicide was the most public of three suicides in her family, and one that affirmed her determination to help others to heal. Bev is a board member of several suicide prevention organizations. She and her coauthor Jean Larch wrote the acclaimed book *Dying to Be Free: A Healing Guide for Families After a Suicide* (Hazelden, 2006). Bev may be contacted through her Web site at www.LivingMatters.com.

Other Great Books from Free Spirit

Too Stressed to Think?
A Teen Guide to Staying Sane When Life Makes You Crazy
by Annie Fox, M.Ed., and Ruth Kirschner
This book is packed with stress-lessening tools teens can use every day to reduce or stop stress and make sound decisions. Includes resources. For ages 12 & up.
$14.95; Softcover; 176 pp.; illust.; 6" x 9"

The Power to Prevent Suicide
A Guide for Teens Helping Teens (Updated Edition)
by Richard E. Nelson, Ph.D., and Judith C. Galas,
Foreword by Bev Cobain, R.N.,C.
Updated with new facts and resources, this book helps teens recognize the risk and respond appropriately. It describes the warning signs and spells out the steps of reaching out to a friend in danger. It also suggests ways for teens to help themselves when they're feeling stressed or depressed. For ages 11 & up.
$13.95; Softcover; 128 pp.; 6" x 9"

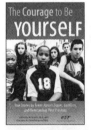

The Courage to Be Yourself
True Stories by Teens About Cliques, Conflicts, and Overcoming Peer Pressure
edited by Al Desetta, M.A., with Educators for Social Responsibility
In 26 searingly honest first-person stories, teens tell how they faced the conflicts in their lives and found the courage to be themselves. Leader's Guide also available. For ages 13 & up.
$13.95; Softcover; 160 pp.; 6" x 9"

The Struggle to Be Strong
True Stories by Teens About Overcoming Tough Times
edited by Al Desetta, M.A., of Youth Communication
and Sybil Wolin, Ph.D., of Project Resilience
Teens tell how they overcame major life obstacles. For ages 13 & up.
$14.95; Softcover; 192 pp.; 6" x 9"

Life Lists for Teens
Tips, Steps, Hints, and How-Tos for Growing Up, Getting Along, Learning, and Having Fun
by Pamela Espeland
More than 200 powerful self-help lists cover topics ranging from health to cyberspace, school success to personal safety, friendship to fun. *Life Lists* is a ready source of guidance for all kinds of situations. For ages 11 & up.
$11.95; Softcover; 272 pp.; 6" x 9"

When a Friend Dies
Revised & Updated Edition
by Marilyn E. Gootman, Ed.D.
Foreword by R.E.M. lead singer Michael Stipe
The death of a friend is a wrenching event for anyone at any age. Teens especially need help coping with this painful loss. This sensitive book provides advice that is gentle, non-preachy, and compassionate. For ages 11 & up.
$9.95; Softcover; 128 pp.; 5" x 7"

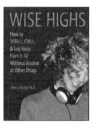

Wise Highs
How to Thrill, Chill, & Get Away from It All Without Alcohol or Other Drugs
by Alex J. Packer, Ph.D.
Describes more than 150 ways to feel really, really good—naturally, safely, and creatively. From breathing and meditation to exercise and sports, gardening, music, and games, these are "highs" that can change teens' lives without leaving them dull, burned out, or hung over. For ages 13 & up.
$15.95; Softcover; 264 pp.; illust.; 7¼" x 9¼"

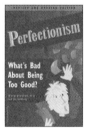

When Something Feels Wrong
A Survival Guide About Abuse
by Deanna S. Pledge, Ph.D.
Teens who have been physically, sexually, and/or emotionally abused need information and support to start the healing process. Written by a psychologist who has worked with abused kids and teens, this realistic, empowering book offers positive ways to deal with a history of abuse. For ages 13 & up.
$14.95; Softcover; 224 pp.; illust.; 6" x 9"

Perfectionism
What's Bad About Being Too Good?
by Miriam Adderholdt, Ph.D., and Jan Goldberg
Perfectionism is a problem for many teens today. This book helps teens discover if they're perfectionists, explore reasons why, and try different ways to ease up on themselves. It gives adults insights into how their behavior and expectations can contribute to perfectionism in kids they parent and teach. For ages 13 & up.
$12.95; Softcover; 136 pp.; illust.; 6" x 9"

To place an order or to request a free catalog of Self-Help for Kids® and Self-Help for Teens® materials, please write, call, email, or visit our Web site:

Free Spirit Publishing Inc.
217 Fifth Avenue North • Suite 200 • Minneapolis, MN 55401
toll-free 800.735.7323 • local 612.338.2068
fax 612.337.5050 • help4kids@freespirit.com • www.freespirit.com